I Served With Hitler
in the Trenches

I Served With Hitler in the Trenches

In the Field, 1914–1918

Hans Mend

Translated by Graham Harris

Frontline Books

First published in Great Britain in 2022 by
Frontline Books
An imprint of
Pen & Sword Books Ltd
Yorkshire – Philadelphia

Copyright © German text Hans Mend 2022
Copyright © English translation Graham Harris 2022

ISBN 978 1 39901 001 6

The rights of Hans Mend to be identified as Author and Graham Harris as Translator of this work have been asserted by them in accordance with the Copyright, Designs and Patents Act 1988.

A CIP catalogue record for this book is
available from the British Library.

All rights reserved. No part of this book may be reproduced or transmitted in any form or by any means, electronic or mechanical including photocopying, recording or by any information storage and retrieval system, without permission from the Publisher in writing.

Typeset by Mac Style
Printed and bound in the UK by CPI Group (UK) Ltd,
Croydon, CR0 4YY.

Pen & Sword Books Limited incorporates the imprints of Atlas, Archaeology, Aviation, Discovery, Family History, Fiction, History, Maritime, Military, Military Classics, Politics, Select, Transport, True Crime, Air World, Frontline Publishing, Leo Cooper, Remember When, Seaforth Publishing, The Praetorian Press, Wharncliffe Local History, Wharncliffe Transport, Wharncliffe True Crime and White Owl.

For a complete list of Pen & Sword titles please contact

PEN & SWORD BOOKS LIMITED
47 Church Street, Barnsley, South Yorkshire, S70 2AS, England
E-mail: enquiries@pen-and-sword.co.uk
Website: www.pen-and-sword.co.uk

Or

PEN AND SWORD BOOKS
1950 Lawrence Rd, Havertown, PA 19083, USA
E-mail: Uspen-and-sword@casematepublishers.com
Website: www.penandswordbooks.com

Contents

Foreword	vii
Introduction	ix
Mobilisation	1
In the Heavy Cavalry Barracks	2
With the List Regiment	2
March to the Front	4
Death of Colonel List	6
With Adolf Hitler in Wytschaete	12
Bethlehem's Farm	13
Static Warfare	15
In the Monastery at Messines	16
Christmas, 1914 with Adolf Hitler	21
1915	28
Burst of Fire at Neuve Chapelle	41
Front Line at Fromelles	51
9 May 1915	58
Army Report, 9 May 1915	66
Long Hans	79
Chateau La Vallée	82

25 September 1915	83
Night Bath in the Castle Moat at Ligny	87
Experiences in Wavrin	88
Penetration of the English	90
Winter in Flanders	93
Trip into the Communications Zone	96
Christmas, 1915 in Fournes	99
New Year's Eve, 1915	102
1916	105
An Unsuccessful Hunt	107
Medical Service	109
Farewell from the Regiment	110
Battle of 19 and 20 July at Fromelles	112
Homecoming	116

Foreword

There is a yawning gap in literature about Adolf Hitler. When, in the post-war era, Adolf Hitler's star appeared in the political sky, no one asked where he had come from. His thoughts and words were prophecies, to one a portent, to many others his views and morality were infinitely incomprehensible. In the meantime, Adolf Hitler became leader of approximately 10 million Germans who were exposed to his words. As economic and political necessity intensified, his supporters quadrupled. The question of where the new leader comes from is quite understandable. Many want to know where Adolf Hitler was during the war years and what he achieved there.

It is a well-known thing that men who pursue the world war waste no words over it. They simply do their great patriotic duty. It came to be that the glorious List regiment, which set out with Adolf Hitler, suffered such heavy losses there were only a few survivors, which, to a certain extent, mirrors the experiences and activities of Adolf Hitler during this time. After much effort I succeeded in discovering a martyr and a comrade who fought side by side and suffered with Adolf Hitler. However, there was a sense of desolation and emptiness around the old heroic List comrades. Reinforced again and again, commander after commander lost, officers of all ranks dead or badly wounded, best friends and comrades there.

A truly brave horseman and front-line soldier, drawn into the field with five brothers and who lost three of them, broke his silence after more than a decade. These are recollections of a simple soldier, of a horseman through and through. The reputation of this man which, because of his achievements, earned him the name 'The despatch rider of the List regiment', has almost become legendary. These memorable experiences will be described in this book as fully as possible. These accounts form only a small part, with pictures of the positions and localities, of Adolf

Hitler's story, a simple soldier, tirelessly doing his duty, uncomplainingly, as a messenger, day and night, with exemplary heroism.

This book aims to convey to the German people small extracts about the German Fatherland from the unknown years of comrade-in-arms Adolf Hitler. These pages are written to establish the truth.

Introduction

In this book I hope to enlighten the German nation about Hitler as a front-line soldier. As a friend, I often had the opportunity of hearing his comments about the war, observing his bravery and becoming familiar with his exemplary qualities.

In writing this book I definitely do not seek to serve any party or other and my views are independent. The book is solely about the soldier Adolf Hitler, who over time I formed a comradeship with only the front-line soldier understands. Fervent love for his greater Fatherland compelled him to incredible achievements in the field. It was long decided for him who the real enemy of our people was, and still is. He has fought persistently to the present day against this destructive power.

In Germany, as abroad, there are contradictory judgements of Adolf Hitler. Many of his opponents see in him a political agitator, who smuggled himself into Germany after the war to set himself up as a political messiah. I want to prove here that he was the same in the field as today, brave, fearless, outstanding.

The Author

Mobilisation

It was 28 July 1914 when I received my call-up in Frankfurt. I was a young reservist, had served actively in the 2nd Uhlan regiment in Ansbach and, as result, had to report there in three days' time. However, I lay in hospital following a serious fall from a horse, which is why I could not comply immediately with my call-up; my injuries had still not healed.

Despite the greatest difficulties, I, nevertheless, pursued my aim of joining the cavalry. With the heart and soul of a professional horseman I wanted to go into the field with my Uhlans. Like iron to a magnet, so my regiment pulled together, and even the strongest impediment could not keep me from my path. I set out ignoring all pain.

Our regiment was full of reservists and civilians from the various locations, refugees who returned from abroad bearing placards with the message: 'Reservist from England, Belgium, France', there were even Italians among us, whose only concern was to reach their homeland early enough to be able to surrender to their troops. One of them said in good German: 'Do you know that in three days, the Italian fleet is setting sail, I have served in it and must be in Venice in two days.' Unfortunately, the fleet did not have such allies upon its return.

Everyone was excited, both soldiers and civilians, to find themselves in a state of war. Every German carried in their consciousness that their nation would win. We really looked forward to being able to travel free in first class, although we would constantly swap seats and standing places with each other. In our compartment a lady was travelling with her daughter who appeared to belong to high society, and I assumed they were Italian aristocrats. She had a wonderful heraldic ring, manufactured in gold, on one of her fingers. She regretted that we had to go to war and told us that she was from Ostend and was travelling to Switzerland. I asked her whether she was Italian or Swiss. 'That's doesn't matter' was her answer. Her daughter let slip the remark 'We are from Paris', and, as a consequence, they had a long unwanted stop at the next checkpoint.

Next morning, I reached my garrison and reported to 2nd Bavarian Uhlan regiment: it was ready to march. I could not go with them as the regimental doctor refused to declare me fit for duty after inspecting my injury. What to do now? I drew up my plan quickly. I tried my luck again with the 2nd Bavarian heavy cavalry regiment in Munich. On the way to the station a schoolfriend told me that, yesterday, my five brothers had gone into the field. 'And I can end up anywhere', I thought wrathfully. I departed full of expectation and reported with my military pass to the Munich station commander. Nobody knew that I had been declared unfit for duty when I had arrived in Munich. At the station entrance I encountered Mr Erzellenz from the military service, who knew me previously. I stated my request and Erzellenz promised to do what he could for me.

In the Heavy Cavalry Barracks

The next morning I reported to the regimental office of the 1st heavy cavalry regiment and, thanks to the recommendations of Erzellenz, was accepted and able to break in horses. No further investigation took place and I took care to say nothing about my injury. As one of the few Uhlans among the Swiss riders, I had to swallow some jibes, for in peace the tradition holds: 'My own regiment is the most splendid and best'. My sergeant was not good at speaking to me and always allocated me horses to ride that were not the best in the troop.

The horses that remained in the barracks were understandably in a bad way, like horses with saddle aversion, runaways or stayers. Often, when such an animal was assigned, I heard the remark: 'Only he who rides with a heavy cavalryman is ashamed of an Uhlan.' After some weeks of tiring service I was appointed despatch rider for the List regiment for 2nd and 6th heavy cavalry, composed entirely of active serving men.

With the List Regiment

My task for the time being was breaking in the officers' service horses, which was no small task, for some days I had six to eight horses to ride. The regiment consisted mainly of volunteers, mostly students, with whom I got on well. From none did I hear remarks which suggested what they hoped to do when they were back.

We had all become friends when on 20 October 1914 the division marched off in the direction of Lechfeld for a three-day battle. In Bavarian Swabia, where we set up quarters, more horses were purchased for the regiment, and my expertise with horses came in useful.

The following Thursday I passed the village blacksmith. A gypsy cantered up to the blacksmith on a wonderful grey and appeared to me intent on selling the animal. It was a definite cavalry horse, with a beautiful saddle position and good legs, although exhausted and underfed. Straightaway I was interested in the horse and I decided to speak to our veterinary surgeon about buying her for the regiment.

Some hours later I visited the blacksmith and asked whether he had struck a deal with the gypsy. The blacksmith said: 'I have bought the horse without a guarantee, it has been lame on the front leg for half a year and is not to be put into harness, but I will find a buyer straightaway.' I examined the horse's legs but could not find any damaged tendons or hoof disease. On my request the master gave me permission to try out the horse; quickly I fetched my saddle and rode her in free, open country. After riding I already knew what the horse was missing, she was a 'passer' which meant it rode along on the wrong foot and thus displayed an unequal gait. Through horsemanship I forced her into a normal step. To be on the safe side, I went back via the blacksmith and lead the horse by the rein because, if the blacksmith saw how the horse was with the rider, he would certainly have demanded a higher price. This was all in the interest of the regiment. The blacksmith came to me asking, 'Is she very lame?' 'Yes, she is still lame but she can still be used as a service horse.' Some hours later the horse was purchased by the regiment at a cheap price and was sent to my quarters as my despatch horse.

In Bavarian Swabia, I encountered Adolf Hitler for the first time. I did not know him, but in passing he stood out because of his energetic expression and individual nature. I considered him highly academic as he listened to so many of the List regiment. The next day I saw him for the second time, as he played around with his weapon. He viewed it with great delight, which I had to laugh at in secret.

March to the Front

After sharpshooting in Lechfield, we were entrained and travelled towards the enemy. Nobody in the List regiment suspected how many would come to rest under foreign soil over the next two weeks. Joy shone from every eye that the waiting was finally over – we were on our way. We travelled through Württemberg, Baden and the beautiful Rhineland; at each stop we were very well looked after, the people of the Rhine putting their greatest hope in us Bavarians, and many delicacies, cigars and cigarettes were passed to us by the friendly young ladies of the Rhine. Enthusiastically we took in the beautiful district because many had not seen the Rhine before. 'The French cannot come here. Even if we all have to perish.'

Towards evening our train passed the border at Autumn Valley. We saw immediately from the faces of the Belgian population that we were now in enemy territory. Outside and around Liège the first traces of the war were evident: burned out houses, torn up streets, trees shot to pieces. We reached Brussels the following afternoon and at midnight on the journey to Lille we heard the first thunder of cannon.

The troops lay snoozing in the train, pressed up tightly together, as we despatch riders prepared our horses in camp. My horse was the only one that was comfortable and lay next to me; I used its neck as a pillow and we must have both slept well, for when I awoke, it was already daylight and a comrade told me that we were outside Lille.

At 8 o'clock we unloaded; we were received by terrible cannon thunder but the morale of the troops was good, one could clearly notice the gallows humour of many which hid the initial fear. We despatch riders and combat staff were accommodated in the hippodrome, while the battalions took over most schools and other buildings.

When I went, in the afternoon, with an order for Regimental Sergeant Umann, now director of the party publishing company and Eher's successor, who had set up his office in a classroom, I again encountered Adolf Hitler. He was close to Lille high school, which, in previous battles, had been shot up. Hitler looked at the devastation keenly with a comrade. Weapon in hand, helmet on his head, with moustache hanging down, he was the picture of a real farm worker. As an active soldier, I recognised in him immediately a born soldier and thought to myself, with him we can succeed.

An orderly, who had known Adolf Hitler longer, answered my question as to whether he knew this Austrian infantryman, a fine chap and, on my question as to why an Austrian was serving in a Bavarian regiment, he answered, 'As far as I know, he was supposed to report to the Austrian consulate upon mobilisation, but went instead to the Austrian king, who personally gave him permission to serve in the Bavarian army.' To my further question as to what Hitler's job was, he replied that he could not say, but as far as he knew, he could do anything.

We stayed for some days in the centre of Lille and during this time we had the opportunity to get to know the civilian population better; they were certainly not hostile, especially the beautiful Lille girls who knew how to flirt with German boys. When I asked the daughter of a Lille citizen why she could not be angry with German soldiers, she answered, 'I like German soldiers a lot. You know, sir, love knows no country.'

On the last day before our departure for the front, I rode my horse once again to test out whether I could rely on a hard ride. Good care and rich feed during the last ten days had brought an animal like this to its peak as I had sensed while riding, my 'girl' was now stable, she went like a gazelle under me. In these last days I romped around the suburbs of Lille on my horse and there were admiring and curious looks and comments like, 'That is a French horse. Perhaps it has been stolen by the Germans.'

On this ride I encountered my Regimental Colonel, List. He stopped me, 'Are you despatch rider Mend?' 'Yes, sir.' 'I need a reliable despatch, my adjutant is not good with horses, from now on you are to be at my disposal.' 'Yes, Colonel'. I was pleased and stayed by his side from this time on.

The next day, at midnight, the regiment marched through the Lille forts around St Andrée and through Belgian-French Comines to Wervik. There we had quarters but there was no water and it wasn't until nearly evening that my horse was able to get a drink at a farm. We were not there long as a Prussian hussar thundered over with the order to clear the farm as heavy English fire threatened, and we had hardly got 200yd away when the first 35s exploded.

I could not wait until after the English firing had stopped in the evening to see the civilians, the inhabitants of the farm. Unfortunately, the shells had done their bloody work. The husband lay on the stairs, the wife with the little child horribly silent in a pit, I could find no trace of the old woman, probably she lay under the ruins of the house. Searching further I found two officer orderlies with their horses, some distance away a third horse was horribly whinnying with pain, whereupon I put it out of its misery. My own horse became very unsettled at this and attempted to flee. For the first time I saw the terror of war.

Toward evening the regiment stood on high alert. We fetched straw and prepared the camp for the night. My 'girl', who I had tied to a tree, woke me after a short sleep, while she sniffed around my face. I knew what she wanted and, despite the strictest orders, I removed the heavily packed saddle and immediately made her comfortable on it at my side.

The morning was for many of my comrades their last awakening. The sky flamed red from the fire from shot-up villages. The order to move off had arrived. I rode at the head of the regiment, in order to look for Colonel List. Among the orderlies I noticed Adolf Hitler. He had moved a bit ahead, a smile on his lips. When I saw Hitler for the first time, I thought what would this slight man do if he should have to carry a fieldpack? I had changed my view. For, as it later transpired, there only a very few in the regiment as resilient and fit as Hitler. With unbelievable toughness he endured the greatest strains and never allowed weakness to show.

The combat orderlies to whom Hitler also belonged were much more exposed to enemy fire than the companies themselves, because, while the latter could again and again take cover on the ground, the orderlies were always on the move with despatches, and I am amazed even to this day that Adolf Hitler was fortunate enough to survive this.

Death of Colonel List

The next day the regiment marched in the direction of Wytschaete and was deployed at Béthune. But, after a few days, we had to be pulled out of the position. Complete companies were torn to pieces. One non-commissioned officer battalion commander, Regimental Doctor Rühl, took over command of the regiment. Not far from the firing line, behind a small hill, I stopped by the supply depot when I got the order to ride to Colonel List at Hollebeke chateau. I looked on the map for Hollebeke chateau and rode off. The road over there was shot-up by the English with shells of all types. I chased away on my horse across trenches, fenced in pastures, hedges. It was as if the good animal knew it was a matter of life and death. Everywhere fallen soldiers lay around and I saw a number of things that I would not want to describe. The castle was already greatly weakened by English shelling. In the rooms many pieces of English equipment were to be found. To all intents and purposes they had fled in a hurry. Colonel List was talking with an officer of the Saxon troops, who had dug a trench at Hollebeke chateau, when I reported. My commander made the Saxons aware that they should dig the trenches deep as the ground around Hollebeke would probably come under heavy English artillery fire again. A cheerful Saxon answered the colonel, 'Colonel, I am as ready as if today we were gathering for Ascension Day.' Colonel List nodded and said nothing more about it. Even to my question as to how our troops were, he gave no answer, he just looked at me and turned away. Suddenly he asked, 'Mend, where have you put your horse?' 'In a room behind the castle, Colonel.' 'Get ready and ride back, perhaps you will find my batman, he should come to me with the horses.'

I ran around the castle to my 'girl'. As soon as I got there, however, three heavy English shells struck the building. I could not see anything else, or even breathe because of the dust. With the greatest effort I shoved my horse out backwards and also heard calls for help from the other side of the castle. One shell had struck a group of Saxons who were busy digging the trench. Some radio operators immediately sprang to the aid of the wounded. At once one of them cried, 'The Bavarian Colonel is also dead!' In my terror I left my horse standing and sprinted over to Colonel List. He was already covered with a canvas sheet. I lifted it up and just saw the blood flowing from his mouth. I could not comrpehend that our brave commander, who was a true leader of his troops, was no more.

I immediately left Hollebeke and set off to look for Colonel List's batman. He was not at the supply depot, where most of the batmen stopped. I rode up again to the castle and encountered him on the way there. 'Has anything happened to Colonel List?' When I told him that he had fallen at Hollebeke, he cried like a child.

One of the most dangerous places for Adolf Hitler, which he had to visit as combat orderly, was the narrow pass in Wytschaete. When I arrived there during the battle with a message, I saw a terrible sight. The company was dug in on the embankment on both sides, to a certain extent protected from shell splinters. Lieutenant Schmidt lay critically ill in a foxhole, his body copper-coloured with fever. His men stretched a canvas sheet over him and by summoning up his last strength he held his company together and gave orders.

The narrow passage was strewn with the dead and wounded. On 2 November alone 119 were counted dead there. From here Adolf Hitler had to deliver his messages. How he succeeded then, forcing himself through the incessant artillery fire, is still incomprehensible to me today. The few minutes in which I was stopped in the narrow passage almost cost me and my horse our lives, for while I waited to give my message to the critically ill lieutenant, who was the only officer present in the narrow passage, an enemy salvo struck and killed several comrades. As the message was not intended for Lieutenant Schmidt, he refused to accept it and sent me to Groene Linde. I was glad to be allowed to leave the narrow passage, in which there was only blood and dead and dying comrades. Hardly had I mounted and set off than a second salvo struck the narrow passage, which, from the testimony of one surviving comrade, killed seventeen men. Under the terrible fire from Hollebeke to Groene Linde my horse drove on, avoiding every obstacle. When I reached the place, most of the houses stood in flames. In the wall of one house stood a 35.5cm shell, which had not exploded. Nearby on the street lay shot-up vehicles with dead soldiers and horses. A despatch rider galloped past at top speed. His horse had been shot and was bleeding profusely. While I was getting my bearings on the map, a motorcycle despatch rider arrived and seeing me, asked where he could find orderlies. Some 100m from Groene Linde an artilleryman lay with his badly wounded horse. The horse was in fact dead and if the artillery man was not given medical assistance he would die. I rode immediately to one of our batteries, which was firing at Groene Linde, and advised the doctor to send some orderlies with a stretcher to the artilleryman. Adolf Hitler had, on this day, achieved amazing things and was one of those decorated after the battle with the Iron Cross, Second Class.

On 4 November we returned again to Wervik and I looked for my old quarters. The people had thought us dead. 'Today, I prayed at Mass, that all those good boys who were at our house, had not been shot and will return', said the daughter of the people I was billeted with. The mother gave up her bed for me, so that I could change and have a good sleep. They themselves made do with a straw mattress on the floor, these blonde Flemish people who thought of us as nothing like the Barbarians that other people liked to pass us off as.

After some days of rest in Wervik, we went back to Comines with the 6th reserve division, and there all the quarters were occupied. We spent the night out in the open, soldiers and horses suffering in the damp, cold, autumn weather and many becoming ill. Continuously troops pushed through the place, and I once heard a local civilian comment, 'We believe in Germany there is a soldier factory.' A Belgian dentist remarked to me, 'Before the German army marched in here, they said that it would be largely destroyed on the Marne and now they come to us in their legions.' He sighed and said to himself, 'My god, our poor Fatherland is lost.'

The population were not as inwardly hostile as we had expected. Mainly small businesspeople and the poorer population came to us to trade. Our troops happily put money in their pockets and some shopkeepers made a fortune from our garrison.

One day Adolf Hitler approached me in front of the spinning mill in which, after the move, the various troops from the majority of our regiments were accommodated. He had put on the message bag and, with his quick, purposeful walk, you could assume that he brought with him an important report about the situation regarding the shelling. His uniform, particularly at the knees, was thick with clay. While I still contemplated what he might encounter in the forward position, although the regiment lay at rest, he disappeared through the gate in the spinning mill.

My horse was suffering from a heavy cold, as once again I spent the night out in the open. I actively went to look for quarters. The last house on the Comines–Warneton road, quite near the cemetery, was a cafe called 'The Gravedigger'. I wanted to drink a cup of coffee but had to force my way through soldiers.

It was often like this on the march to or return from the front. Many took the necessary courage from several schnapps before they marched to the firing. Madame Culier, the owner, never left anything to chance, she earned a pretty penny from us soldiers; her beautiful daughter served at the bar and many a jealous look flew from one to another if she talked a bit longer than normal with a comrade. In the kitchen there was always a little warm place and she took many a poor devil, wet through from the front, out into the kitchen, so that he could dry off and warm up.

'I should have my quarters here', I thought to myself and was lucky. After some toing and froing, my French-speaking abilities assisting me, I acquired a little room and my horse a warm stable together with Mr Hugo, the gravedigger.

One evening when I was walking across the Ypres Canal bridge, I got two messages from Dr Rühl. One was to the regimental doctor of 17th Bavarian reserve infantry regiment in the field hospital at Comines; the second was to the divisional doctor in Warneton. I returned, saddled up my horse and rode first to the field hospital at Comines. It was dark when I gave my message to an orderly there. While I was waiting for an answer, heavy calibre English shells struck the field hospital, killing many wounded as well as some Belgian monks, who had remained in the converted monastery. Above me fell a shower of bricks and dust.

The inner monastery presented a hideous sight. Of the wounded lying on the ground, there remained not one alive. The whole room was yellow from sulphur shells. Nuns carried their dead sisters past and prayed. Despite all the trouble, I could no longer find the orderly who was supposed to bring me an answer.

I mounted up and rode with my second message to Warneton. The night was dark and only with difficulty could I make my way through the streets with my horse, for vehicles of all types, munitions columns and equipment wagons which were bringing material for the reinforcement of the positions at the front were accumulated here. Now and again some lights could be seen in the shot-up houses; everything made a ghostly impression. To my enquiry to an orderly I got the answer that the divisional doctor was at the dressing station. Handing over my message, I looked again at the church, in which many wounded lay illuminated by faint candlelight, groaning and wracked with pain. Having returned to my quarters I fell into a deep sleep from which Mr Hugo had to wake me the next day.

Daily at daybreak, the kilometre-long columns of vehicles moved to the sections of the front, bringing material there for its reconstruction. The French vehicles, stuck in the middle of the wrecked streets, were in such bad condition that it sometimes appeared impossible to even get forward with a horse and cart. Deep holes were encountered on the side roads, so that the vehicles often got stuck in them or overturned. In the ditches lay various vehicles, cars, munitions wagons, bicycles and such like.

One evening I happened upon a field kitchen which had had the good fortune to avoid the more dangerous position between Warneton and Osterwerne: but its precious contents was being distributed all along the ditches and circulating the most marvellous odours. The officer responsible for the kitchen addressed the driver with words which were scarcely to be found in a German dictionary. He knew too well how he would be received in the position if he were to arrive with empty pans. With united strength we succeeded in making the goulash stove quick and efficient again. The cauldron was heated up and filled once more.

'Franz, if you throw the cooking pot into the ditch again, then I shall shoot you,' was the warning with which the non-commissioned officer dismissed the driver. Scenes such as these were repeated now and again on this street.

An overturned munitions wagon at the entrance to the town bore witness to the heavy shelling of recent days. Four horses lay terribly torn up next to the wagon with glazed eyes and tongues hanging out. In the monastery of Wytschaete I found Colonel Engelhardt, the first successor to the brave Colonel List, lying on a bed in the cellar, badly wounded. Around him stood some orderlies. When he heard that I had a message for him, he bade me enter, accepted it and gave me some cigars, before dismissing me.

In the greatest pain, Colonel Engelhardt did his duty as commander, and if today there are Germans who belittle the achievements of our front-line officers, I would like to point out that most of our officers went through the same stresses as us and to their last breath upheld their responsibilities.

With Adolf Hitler in Wytschaete

Our regimental headquarters was in the monastery at Wytschaete, and the orderlies and despatch riders went in and out of there daily. It is unbelievable what was achieved by them in those days, and whoever came out of this witches' cauldron uninjured was a matter of luck. Among these few was Adolf Hitler. One bright day, under heavy shell and machine-gun fire, which troops in their foxholes hardly daring to lift their heads, he was moving around with messages from the monastery to the front line. When I happened to ride towards him, he laughed at me, as if he wanted to say, 'Don't get any grand ideas, just because you are a despatch rider. We achieve just as much as you!'

Once I was there as he was having a dispute with another orderly, who spoke of the great dangers the patrols were constantly placed under. Hitler, who could not stand a show-off and who himself never gave an indication even if he was faring badly, said angrily, 'If any of us orderlies were such a chicken like you, the colonel could bring over his own messages. I believe you are suffering from shellshock.'

After days of heavy losses, we moved into Comines and I quartered myself again at Madame Culier's. During these days of rest the first vaccinations were administered and, in fact, in the spinning mill in which the regiment was accommodated earlier. I was given the order to look for replacement Officer Stephan's trench, who was presumed missing, and whose parents wanted to bring their son home. I looked in every trench in our original positions at Becelaere, but in vain. Completely soaked, I came back to Comines just as night was falling and was greeted by terrible screaming in the orderly sergeant's spinning mill. 'If you come immediately for vaccinating, perhaps you will get an extra sausage roasted.' I stood the plaster boxes down, half-frozen and wet through, accepting I should get myself vaccinated. The event was naturally reported to the colonel who in fact the same day spared me the procedure, but the next they caught up with me.

Bethlehem's Farm

We were now under the third Regimental Commander, First Lieutenant Betz. At night the regiment was put into the left of Messines at Bethlehem's Farm. After the English had firmly entrenched themselves on the Kemmelberg and had showered us with shells during the day, we Germans were not up to organising much. The Kemmelberg was a natural fortress and our artillery heavily engaged the enemy. We, in the valley, were subjected to the heaviest fire because the positions in this part of the front were not yet reinforced and our 'Listers' sometimes stood up to their knees in water. When, at night, we moved into the farm as the regiment's quarters, a non-commissioned officer said to me, 'If you want to be alive tomorrow, then come out as quick as possible, as the English batteries have been looking for our positions already all afternoon and many shells have exploded close by us. Today they have already battered the farm with shrapnel'.

We fetched straw bales and barricaded the barn, because a radio operator had already been badly wounded by a rifle bullet. In the early hours First Lieutenant Betz gave me the order to ride to the monastery in Messines and take a message to the artillery position. 'My dear Mend, come back to me again but avoid the streets when possible.' With these words he dismissed me.

Shot after shot struck the stone streets and although my commander had only marked two crosses on my message, my horse chased there as if it was six. At the foot of the hill, on whose top Messines lay, I let my brave animal have a breather and then set off again. The officer, to whom I gave my message, was astonished that I had got through this firing without being wounded. 'As long as I ride my horse, nothing will happen, she is my talisman.'

It was a bright day when I got back to Bethlehem's Farm. The despatch riders who, days before were ready to take the baton at the farm, got the message to stop in Messines monastery in order to be at the disposal of the battalion commanders; only Hitler, Schmidt, myself and some other orderlies, some nurses and the doctor remained with the commander. Two nurses took over the cook's office. An abandoned pig which was running around was supposed to be slaughtered but would not allow itself to be caught; it fled from the farm out into the street and so it did not evade being roasted, the cook shot after the escapee. Because of this lack of care our enemy noticed that there were still troops in the farm and a short time later the farm came under fire. The first shells struck a shed and immediately killed more radio operators. We wanted to bury the dead straightaway and dug a few graves in the garden, while the doctor, Fischer, and Adolf Hitler made crosses out of wood for the dead. The doctor came to us and said: 'I think we should dig a few more graves straightaway in case none of us survive this hell. It is possible that I am now making my own cross?'

First Lieutenant Betz came into the garden to see the dead and gave me a message for Warneton. On the way I heard shell blasts and recognised, from the pillars of smoke, that they had exploded in the yard. At full gallop I rode to Warneton, handed over my message and returned at the same pace. When I rode into the burning yard, First Lieutenant Betz was stood there with a grim face and gave orders to the survivors. I reported to him, 'Order carried out.'

The brim of his cap was lowered and an epaulette had been torn away by a shell splinter. He went into the stables and standing at the door he called me, 'Mend, shoot the wounded horses!' I fetched the wounded animals out one after another and relieved them from their pain by a shot to the head. In the barn lay many dead comrades, among them Dr Fischer, he really had made his own cross. The nurses were busy bandaging the wounded and the orderlies were taking over the burying of the dead in the garden.

How Adolf Hitler came out of this hell is still a puzzle to me today. All I know is that he was present at the farm and had slung on his canteen, weapon on his arm, expecting orders in the barn. Whether during the shooting he had been sent away with a message or was spared by the shells, I do not know. Some days later I was chatting in Messines about events, expressing my amazement that I was still alive, and laughingly called to him, 'Hey, there's no bullet with your name on it!' He answered with a smile.

When we were later in our quarters, we often thought of the terrible days at Bethlehem's Farm.

Static Warfare

Static warfare had begun. Our regimental staff were quartered in the main square in Messines and even the orderlies, including Hitler, had their accommodation there. The little town was completely shot to bits, but as the enemy knew there were troops here, he nonetheless sent his rounds onto this ruined field.

I often admired Regimental Sergeant Umann and his clerk, as they sat writing with the greatest peace in their cellar hole, while above the greatest calibre shells exploded. The quarters of our regimental sergeant looked like a strangely spared island. In the middle of this crater, that was already freshly churned up by shells, this man showed striking courage, doing his duty sufficiently, as self-evidence. Sometimes though he would say to arrivals, 'You have it better than me, here I crouch in this shell-cratered island, I often don't hear or see.'

Calmness and humour were the best companions of our soldiers. In our spare time we played cards and the sound of a harmonica or a piano was heard from many houses. During a heavy bombardment a volunteer played 'To the Fight, Torero' on the piano. I peeped out of the shot-up window, 'Do you still feel like playing, it's going wild outside!' 'Yes, I know, that stimulates me', he said laughing.

I met Adolf Hitler several times a day when he was taking messages. One day when I was returning on the Warneton–Osterwerne road, it was violently shelled. Many poplars that had lined the street lay across it. Riding at a sharp gallop, I saw two infantrymen with message bags coming towards me. I wanted to get away from this street quickly but turned around again and saw how Hitler was gesticulating to his comrade Schmidt and making him aware. They stood there as cool as a cucumber and looked into the air, when the Zeppelin flew over the houses.

In the Monastery at Messines

My current quarters were in the monastery buildings at Messines. This little town was once considered the most well-to-do community in the northern French empire. The sad ruins of its shot-up houses and the abandoned fixtures and fittings of its inhabitants were themselves testament to the luxury and comfort enjoyed by earlier owners. The extended monastery buildings, which previously housed a famous girls' boarding school, did not provide the best accommodation for us, and only the massive tower with its metre-thick walls offered enough cover and since November it had been full of invalids, now badly wounded due to enemy shelling. But like a tough front-line soldier it stood firm, and our orderly team felt safe there, hidden with their wounds and out of danger.

The reasonably bombproof vault of the main building accommodated the various battalion staffs and command positions. Unfortunately, our regiment had to make do with a less-safe place for accommodation.

The monastery stables in which I had accommodated my horse offered not the slightest protection due to the thin walls, so that it was possible for another horse which stood next to mine to be wounded by a rifle bullet and several infantrymen, who had hidden themselves away in the hay and straw above our stables, to be injured by English bullets.

For some days now the English had demonstrated a nervousness which showed itself through frequent armed attacks; today also, when at about 4 o'clock in the afternoon Hitler was taking a message from the regimental doctor's which sent him to the monastery tower. I was just in the process of making coffee for both doctors when, suddenly, a heavy shell struck near the tower; at this my coffee pot flew onto the roof due to the air pressure. The fragments of a mirror were blown into our faces, orderly Merl was thrown to the floor, Dr Rühl was unconscious for a short time and blood flowed from his mouth and nose. Only Staff Sergeant Dir was spared and kept his nerve. 'Mend, the English have smelt your coffee beans', he noted, lighting a cigar.

My first thought was for my horse and on my way to its stable I saw a dead man lying in the yard. Orderlies were just carrying a wounded man into their tower and I was already afraid that it would be Hitler, because just a few minutes before he had left. These were, however, two ambulance drivers. I found my horse standing, bathed in sweat, in the stables, fear showing in her eyes. I stayed with her a while, until she was calmed with stroking and soothing words.

The days and weeks passed for all of us in the most stressful message-carrying conditions, which cost the life of many good comrades. The luckiest among us were glad if they could, even if crazy, sulphur yellow like a canary, with bullet holes in their coats or message pouches, return to their quarters. With steaming coffee or a good spit, the experiences of past days were told with a joke and humour. Adolf Hitler was no killjoy; on the contrary, with his ideas and interjections, he always brought the hut to life – only he never spoke about his achievements.

On a beautiful, cold November morning, I was on the way with a message from Comines to Wytschaete. I collected my pay from the reception of the battalion office and, when I had gone a little way, a howling shell flew over me which almost knocked over my horse. The air pressure was horrible, I was bleeding from the nose and my horse was quite disturbed. We limped to Osterwerne. There I mounted again. When I encountered a munitions wagon, a bearded militia man, a driver from an orderly unit, was praying to a red cross. When I asked him whether he was praying for the dead here, he answered, 'Yes already, but look, there lies a Frenchie who I was supposed to bring here earlier today, badly wounded, from Wytschaete, and it seems to me that he died on the way because he moaned such a lot.' I looked and he showed me the photograph of his family, which he held tightly in his hand, and I saw from it that the poor devil was a father of seven. 'And because I just had time, a few of us wanted to pray for his soul; I don't know whether I can do it today. This morning, a neighbour, who I know from my village, was torn up by a shell splinter. He is lying over there; the one with the red moustache. His foot and the top of his head were ripped off'. While the engineer crossed himself, I moved away and rode at a fast gallop to my destination.

The village of Groene Linde had just been shot up by English shrapnel, so I avoided the main road and took a roundabout way to the monastery where I handed over my message, and then was sent on my way to my regimental staff in Messines. As a consequence of the strong gunfire, it was impossible for me to take the nearest route from Wytschaete to

Messines so I rode back to Osterwerne, and from there, protected by a hill, reached my destination. At the crossroads in Osterwerne, I saw immediately that Adolf Hitler had turned into the street to Messines. At a house at the side of the road, I was stopped by a field gendarme who had an order to prohibit vehicles crossing the street. I recognised him as one of my earlier active regimental comrades and said to him that I was also a second-class messenger and he allowed me to pass.

In a garden at the entrance to Osterwerne stood an anti-aircraft position which the English artillery had long since knocked out and I had hardly reached this position when two English shells struck nearby, and the fragments flew across my head; I galloped off on my horse to get out of range. After a while, I noticed how, at the entrance to Messines, the brickworks lay shot up and that Adolf Hitler had thrown himself to the ground because shrapnel fragments were raining down on him. Due to this bombardment I did not want to pass the place but stayed standing with my horse and observed Hitler. Suddenly he jumped up, although the shots were still exploding over him, and continued on his way at a calmer pace. I thought to myself that the man must have no nerves. I followed him and caught up with him at the Grand Place at Messines where he was talking with another messenger and was laughing as if his last dangerous encounter was fun for him. When I came across him again on the road to the monastery, I said to him jokingly, 'The English made you warm before.' He replied, 'That does not bother me, I experience that every day!'

In the first days of December the weather was stormy and rainy. A regimental orderly bought a message to me, in the monastery, with the order to carry it immediately to Comines. In consideration of the three crosses on the message, I got myself ready immediately because day had already broken, and every minute was precious. When I led my horse from the stables, enemy planes crossed over the yard and although it was an order to take cover during enemy air observation, I, nevertheless, saddled up my horse and bandaged her legs. As I checked the horseshoes just in case they were loose, I heard a voice behind me. I was required to bring my horse immediately into the stable or I would be cut down by 'one'. I deliberately took no notice but took a nail from my saddlebag in order to repair the shoe. Then I got a kick in the side and when I turned around a man was standing behind me. Instead of wearing a uniform, he had a leather waistcoat on so that I could not make out his rank. I asked him whether he had deliberately pushed me with his foot. He answered, 'You, corporal, if you don't go with your horse straight away into the stables, you will get cut down by another one'. But he had hardly pronounced 'cut down' when I threw him into the stable's dungheap. He jumped up and came angrily towards me, but I had already got my sword in my hand; he saw that he would be cut down to size and fled into the cellar vault. I rode out of the monastery to deliver my message and, as it was of the highest importance, I would not have stopped for a general much less someone I didn't recognise, no matter what corps he belonged to. After handing over my message at Division in Comines, I rode slowly back to the monastery at Messines. I had hardly restabled my horse than Staff Sergeant Dir came over to me saying, 'Right then Mend, what have you been up to?! You threw a First Lieutenant into the dungheap did you? I have already sorted out the matter because I know you. Of all things that I have seen, you are a despatch rider that cannot be stopped. Did you really throw him in the dungheap?' I admitted that as he wasn't wearing a uniform, I had thrown him in the pit after he had injured me with his foot. Sergeant Dir laughed, 'It's a shame I didn't see it, that would have been something to behold.' While we were still speaking, the First Lieutenant came up to us, the only difference was that he was now wearing his uniform. He asked me just one question, 'Despatch rider, did you know this morning that I am an officer?' I stood to attention and said, 'How could I know you were an officer without your uniform? It would never occur to me to attack an officer. I regret my actions and I apologise.' When I met the First Lieutenant again, sometime later at La Bassée, we greeted each other warmly, exchanged a cigarette and laughed about the event at Messines.

One day I was sent with a sealed letter from Messines to army headquarters in Lille. Sergeant Major Umann gave me the letter with the instruction to come back as quickly as possible with the answer. Some days before I had noticed that my horse was not quite healthy. She was coughing violently, and I feared for her the whole way in such bad weather. To take the shortest way, I rode via Bethlehem's Farm, Warneton, St Margaret auf der Strasse which leads straight to Lille. It was raining heavily; a cold and raw wind was blowing in my face. I could hardly get through with my horse on these muddy paths. Shell holes were close together and all filled with water. At Bethlehem's Farm I saw, down the street, an infantryman standing with his gun by his feet. From his stance I immediately recognised him as Adolf Hitler. In front of him lay two dead, whom he was apparently interested in. At first, I wanted to ride over to Hitler but when I stopped my horse, enemy shells exploded near to him. He looked round and craned his head as if sniffing a wild danger. But despite the greatest danger to life, he stayed standing by the dead. Once he turned towards me, probably he recognised me and wanted to see how I would get through this field of craters.

The English observers must have seen me for another shell landed nearby. I spurred my horse, which I had only done in dangerous situations, but she did not want to go forwards, the firing became even stronger and shell splinters flew away over me. Suddenly I fell from my horse into a shell hole and only with the greatest difficulty could we work ourselves out. I was standing up to my neck in water. My first worry, naturally, concerned the letter; I fetched it out of my sodden messenger bag and put it under my helmet. The shells, which I had forgotten during my involuntary bath, were striking again and again nearby. I had hardly reached the heights of Warneton when a shower of enemy shells came over me. I felt a violent pain in my face and in my right hand. My horse was also bleeding from the neck. The shrapnel balls were crashing against the fork of the saddle and flew up into my face, while another wounded me in the hand. My horse came through with a small wound in the ventricle. With swollen cheeks and hand, I reached Warneton; there I was quickly dressed and continued on my way to Lille with a bandaged head.

Near to St Margaret my horse became so ill that I had to accommodate her on a farm. A car picked me and in a short time I was able to give my letter to Army Headquarters. When I saw my horse again she was lying in a cold stable, on a hard floor and made a pitiful sight. I prepared a warm, soft camp and laid a sheet over her until she sweated. Next morning, my 'girl' was fit again and at a fast gallop I rode back to Messines. I immediately reported the reasons for my long absence at the Staff Headquarters. In the quarters, I met Adolf Hitler and asked what exactly he had seen yesterday at Bethlehem's Farm. 'I saw the two dead, over which the grass had already grown.' I pointed out to him that it would certainly not have been necessary to put himself in this place unless one wanted to catch moles. Hitler pulled at his moustache as if he wanted to say, 'Despatch rider Mend, don't worry about me.'

Before we separated, he noted again, 'Your bones might still be brought in a canvas sheet to Messines.'

Christmas, 1914 with Adolf Hitler

We had been stood now for weeks in Messines, the weather badly affecting the troops in the trenches, with water sometimes up to the knees. It rained incessantly. Day and night, the men had to stay soaked to the skin in the firing positions and, at the same time, reinforce the trenches. Despite the fact that a lot of material had, since the beginning of this static warfare, been brought up to the trenches, it failed to keep them dry. That superhuman efforts were demanded of the troops is unquestionable. The robust types tolerated these stresses naturally better than those who had no physical demands on them in civilian life.

One small satisfaction for us was that the enemy positions were just as bad as ours because the English also had a lot to put up with in the deluge that penetrated the trenches. They tried once, by opening the floodgates, to put our position under water but our engineers prevented this in the nick of time and stemmed the tide. In short, our troops' situation was not enviable and when I see and hear today how the public is spoilt, I often think how we endured everything at that time. On a bale of straw on a cold floor, soldiers sleep decidedly better than many today in the ultra-modern bedroom. How often have I seen on my message rides soldiers asleep in shell holes with knapsacks on their backs, clothes wet through and if I then called to one or other of them, it was impossible for me to wake them. These was just robust types who put up with even more than horses. I remember a convoy of an artillery regiment, horses and teams, having to bivouac in bad weather in open fields. Many horses died there while drivers bothered little about the weather and the majority felt quite well.

Often, I encountered companies which had been relieved and were marching to their quarters. The water squelched in their boots, their clothes were wet and full of clay, but they sang their soldier's songs.

Christmas came around and many would not have cared, if they had been allowed a little leave to spend Christmas with their families. Wishes of this type were often heard but mostly things worked out differently. Shortly before the celebration, I was chatting with some orderlies, none of whom had been granted their special requests; one was looking forward to parcels, the others would have given up everything just to spend an hour at home on Christmas Eve.

Adolf Hitler stood back and did not concern himself with our conversation for he had little interest in such wishes; he was not interested in receiving parcels which most were looking forward to. Comrades received their parcels and offered to share their splendour with Adolf Hitler, but I noticed that he declined to thank them. He ate his army bread with jam and drank a flask full of tea with it.

'Has that Hitler not received Christmas parcels yet?' asked an orderly, to which he received the answer, 'You won't get anything if you don't give something to anyone.' As I knew that before the war Adolf Hitler had to battle to earn a living from his craft, I could not understand his attitude.

On Christmas Eve I rode to Comines. I didn't have a message to bring at that time but searched the streets for farmhouses to get some milk for Dr Rühl who had stomach trouble. The yards were largely shot-up but I knew that it was only in Comines that farmers were still able to carry on relatively as normal. As I passed through Warneton, I saw in the small battalion cemetery the first little Christmas trees and fir trees fixed to the little wooden crosses; the view from the battalion cemetery and the misty December weather gave a melancholic impression and I rode on through the streets at a quicker pace.

On leaving Warneton I encountered the post wagon of our division stacked high with Christmas parcels and I thought of all the glad faces at the distribution of these gifts of love.

Somewhere down the street was a farm whose tenants were well-known Flemish people. In the garden stood anti-aircraft defences whose crew had taken over the farm as quarters. The tenant recognised me straight away again and I made my request. 'Willingly, my boy, but the soldiers who live here won't allow it.' I made the man understand that it was an order from the commander that milk was to be given to sick troops. He got to work with my bottles in the parlour and when he had filled them up, he bought them back followed by a Prussian sergeant. He yelled at me as to why I came here to fetch milk which they needed themselves for their coffee but when he heard of the commandant's order, he backed down straight away. With the bottles in my saddlebags, I proudly returned to the monastery. About 100m from it, a heavy English shell exploded. I crashed to the floor with my horse. Luckily, the scattering of the exploding shells was ahead of us, otherwise I would have been torn to pieces with my horse, but to the right, on the monastery wall, the heavy shell fragments had torn large holes.

When I went into the monastery, I encountered Hitler with a form in his hand and he said, 'Now this time, you have been lucky!' I said, 'Just like you five minutes ago.'

I was glad to have brought back both my milk bottles intact. Dr Dir grabbed me by the shoulder, looked me in the eyes and said, 'Yes, despatch rider Mend still lives', but when he saw both my bottles, he took them from my hand and I heard him, in painful tones in a side room, say to Dr Rühl, 'Look my friend, our despatch rider Mend, performs miracles!' I got a pair of good cigars and while I spoke to Staff Doctor Dir about the circumstances in which I had got the milk, he informed me that some parcels had been handed in for me. 'There are lavish names on them like Frau von Weinberg, Princess Elizabeth of Hohenlohe-Schillingsfürst, Frau Dr Klemm-Mannheim.' 'Heavens, we must open them straight away then we can smoke a good cigar on Christmas Eve in our hell.' Laughing, I opened the parcels, the contents interesting me less than the letters which Her Highness, Princess Elizabeth, who had known me since I was as a child, had sent. With a bottle of cognac and in the meagre light of a Davy lamp, it was quite cosy in our hell especially since our enemy cousin had adjusted his fire.

Dr Dir was very knowledgeable, and we talked about events of the past and it was not until around midnight that we retired to bed.

When I awoke it was already 8 o'clock in the morning, I moved around the room as softly as I could in order not to disturb Drs Dir and Rühl. I made my way to the stable to my horse who was also laying down and showed no sign of getting up. I went to the Grand Place to the regimental staff to look for Adjutant Eichelsdörfer. Everywhere was as quiet as the grave, no shots to be heard and I was pleased that the people's Christmas was still holy and that the relentless killing had stopped. When I entered the room where the orderlies stayed, I saw Adolf Hitler lying on a rucksack, his helmet next to him and his cartridge pouch buckled on but his boots still quite dirty. In the corner lay a non-commissioned officer. They must not have heard my entrance because there was no sign of life. I could not hide a certain pity for Adolf Hitler and thought to myself that the poor devil does such a lot and doesn't even have anyone at home in Germany who he puts his life on the line for and sacrifices his health. I looked again for the adjutant who I found straight away and gave me permission to rest my horse.

I then made my way to my comrades, the other despatch riders, who had made their quarters in the brickworks. They were despatch riders Langwieder, Wind, Höntsch, Loibl and the Kellner brothers. They were just making some strong coffee and they told me that they were so dreadfully exposed to the enemy artillery fire without protection. Langwieder opened a shutter and showed me a large shell hole behind the house. 'Look here Mend, what the English sent us yesterday as a Christmas present, and over there the shell splinters struck the roof.' Incidentally, they did not express any strong opinions about it and despatch rider Höntsch, a born Saxon, grabbed his harmonica and played it in the most marvellous way. It was very happy there and we spoke of our homes and of experiences in enemy territory. You would almost have thought we were at a church celebration at home and not so close to the barrels of the English guns.

I stayed with them until midday and then made my way to my horse in the monastery, she must have felt well as today she could rest properly without being disturbed by English shells, because when I came into the stable at midday, she didn't want to get up despite my repeated requests so I left her lying there, shook some oats into the nosebag and fastened it to her head.

During the afternoon I wandered about between the shot-up houses of Messines and happened to enter a room where the roof had caved in due to the impact of shells. From under the collapsed ruins a shoe poked out, the size of a woman's shoe which still had the foot in it. It terrified me and I left the miserable home. Soon it began to get gloomy, the evening was misty, and I went back to my quarters. Dr Dir made sure that things went with a swing and that the dismal thoughts which had come to me during the ride back from the dreadfully shot-up place were soon banished.

On Boxing Day, I had to take various letters from the field post office to Comines; the morning was cold and wet and although I aimed to do this without exerting my horse and riding there at a comfortable tempo, so as not to be shot I had to go at a fast trot. I was gripped by frost. A chauffeur on the Warneton–Osterwerne road was dealing with a fault with his car. I helped him a bit and he told me that between the enemy positions English and German troops had been bartering and when this became known, the artillery interrupted these trade relations. I had hardly taken my letters from the field post when I heard, again, the thunder of shelling which our enemy soon answered and, in a short time, there was the greatest barrage which signalled the end of the festive celebrations.

When I arrived in Messines at nightfall, the orderlies told me themselves what the chauffeur had reported in the morning. Our artillery did not tolerate relations between the trenches. I took care of my horse, led her to the stable and went to my camp. The first Christmas of the war was over.

During the Christmas period, no major events occurred on our part of the front, and the troops of our regiments hoped that New Year's Eve would be just as calm so we would at least be able to spend the last evening of the year cheerfully. We relied upon the fact that Tommy would not undertake something or other on New Year's Eve, particularly as the end of the year in England is celebrated more than in Germany. Pessimists, on the other hand, were worried that a surprise attack by the English could be a strong possibility and we had to be careful. In view of the various bottles of rum and cognac which had been received at the monastery in parcels from loving relatives, we looked forward to a good mood on New Year's Eve. Some comrades even had the pious wish to get drunk at New Year.

On New Year's morning I had to get permission from the regimental commander to ride to Comines to shoe my horse there. The Colonel gave me his private letters for the field post in Comines, and another order to his aide who was with the horses in the quarters. I had also received orders from other men in the General Staff. Before I left the staff quarters I went, once again, to Regimental Sergeant Major Umann to notify him that if he needed a despatch rider during the day, he ought to ask one of my colleagues as I would not be coming back until about midnight or the following morning. Sergeant Umann jokingly made some observations about why I was having my horse shoed on New Year's Day; probably I had invited the beautiful Madeleine of Comines, the gravedigger's daughter, for New Year's punch. Then Adolf Hitler entered, he came from the trenches. He was heavily laden and put his bayonetted rifle against the wall. He had a really contented look on his face and was, it seemed to me, in good spirits. Leaving the orderly room, I asked in passing, 'Why have you come here again today?' At this, he jumped to the side, picked up his helmet, bowed to the floor with a mischievous look on his face and said, 'May I wish the immortal horseman of Messines a good New Year.' I wanted to give him a kick for this comment, but he leapt swiftly aside and made further bows in front of me. Of course, he knew that in civilian life I was a professional horseman and had worked in the highest circles. I replied with some strong flattery and went on my way. On the ride to the monastery, I thought to myself, 'This Adolf Hitler, as serious as he sometimes is, at a given moment becomes a joker.' Half an hour later, at the Grand Place of Messines, I saw Hitler again. I just wanted him to get out of the way, but he had already seen me and addressed me again as respectfully as in the regimental quarters. My comrades said to me with a laugh when they witnessed this curious greeting, 'Right, despatch rider, you don't realise that Hitler is laughing at you.' I shook my head in derision; he has not had a good day today as he made the same face as when he went laughing into the cellar. He knows already that I am no creep and willingly have fun with him.

At the entrance to Warneton, a smithy had installed in one of the last remaining houses some sort of temporary set-up. I asked him whether he would shoe my horse. In a Swabian dialect came the answer, 'Oh yes, I can do that but you must wait here, I must only use the right kind of shoes.' He busied himself in a luggage wagon and bought over a pair of large shoes to nail to my horse. These were suitable for a carthorse but not for the small hooves of my thoroughbred Hungarian horse. When I made him aware that, under no circumstances, should my horse have such heavy shoes fitted, the smithy threw the shoes in anger into the street and advised me to have the Devil shoe my horse. Above all, he had talked himself out of business; he would have shoed more horses in his village blacksmith's if I had been someone younger and more inexperienced. I clearly gave him to understand that I had no intention of him shoeing my thoroughbred. As he wasn't getting his own way he became aggressive and he would have thrown red-hot horseshoes at my head if I had not quickly mounted my horse and made off.

In Comines I soon found a cavalry smithy with whom my horse was perfectly shoed. As it began to get dark, I rode to Comines to take care of my orders. In the streets I heard the soldiers wishing each other a happy New Year, and in the cafes they were having a great time. They were full of German troops who had already started their New Year celebrations.

Also, with the civilian population there was a notable improvement in mood. Having been living together with the German troops, they had reached the conclusion that the Germans were not people-eaters. Sometimes a touching scene was observed when the old Home Guard carried such a small French child in their arms that the lad or lass held tightly to the beard of the German Home Guard. In the meantime, in Belgian Comines I reached the house of the gravedigger, my earlier quarters. Upon my arrival, I looked through the window from my horse. The room was full of Prussian engineers. All of them were already cheerful and singing Rhine songs. I asked a few soldiers coming out to call Madam Culier. They must have said it to her daughter who was at the bar because after a few minutes Madeleine came out and welcomed me joyfully. I rode through the gate into the back of the house and was just in the process of looking for my torch in the saddlebag, when I heard my name called by Madam Culier. She greeted me happily and Monsieur Culier came as well. They had thought something had happened to me. Now they bid me to go into the kitchen and Monsieur Culier promised to arrange a warm stable for my horse. Madeleine busied herself with making coffee; she pressed me to her breast and told me she had prayed for my soul at Mass. Surprised, I asked why she was dressed in black, and she told me amid tears that her cousin had fallen in love with a German soldier and the latter had died some weeks ago. Out of grief over the loss of her beloved, her cousin sought death in the Ypres Canal.

Hardly had I sat down by the fire than, probably as a consequence of the change in temperature, I felt a violent toothache. The whole family took care of me, I got warm towels around the head and camomile tea, but nothing helped. Madeleine fetched a Belgian dentist who was known as a good tooth-puller, but he couldn't see anything amiss with my teeth. When around midnight the pain became unbearable, Madeleine led me outside the village to the house of an old man. On our knock, we heard a grumble from within; my companion explained in Flemish why we had come to him so late: 'Come in poor boy', said the old man and opened the door to us. A dog approached us angrily, but the old man kicked him, and, with a howl of pain, he hid behind the fire. I now had to sit down on a chair in front of a crucifix. From the ceiling of the room the man fetched a bundle of herbs, tore some corn and made a mustard paste from it. Then he stepped towards the crucifix, crossed himself and smeared the roof of my mouth with this mysterious mixture. Like a battle victim, I followed all his instructions and, after a few minutes, I felt relief from the pain. Delighted, we gave the old man a coin and returned to the cafe. We found the room empty; all the soldiers had returned to their quarters. Around the warm fireplace I now drank New Year's punch with the Culier family, my toothache had disappeared, and I made up for what I had missed because of it. It was already 2 in the morning when we retired. Madeleine had prepared my little room and laid a hot brick in my bed.

1915

Bright and lively, I got ready in the morning, said goodbye to the people I was billeted with who just wanted to go to Mass, and, accompanied by their good wishes, I rode into the new year.

At the crossroads in Osterwerne, English shells were falling on a farm. Here, a Bavarian battery which the Tommies had sought long ago was entrenched. The many shell craters close to the hidden gun were proof of this. Judging by the shouts, the battery must have received a direct hit. Two orderlies hurried through the garden with a stretcher.

In Messines, I turned off the direct route to reach the monastery. Even here, bullets whistled around my ears. On the side of a mountain stood a second battery in preparation; I saw the fresh shell holes. The gunners looked concerned. The bearded captain stood next to them like a tower of strength and gave his orders in rousing tones. The gunners carried out each one exactly.

Having arrived at the monastery, I stabled my horse and went to the orderlies. At the door of the dayroom, I spoke with replacement Officer Feistle. Through the doors I heard the orderlies discussing political issues loudly. I heard Adolf Hitler's voice clearly among them; he must have been in a verbal battle with his opponent for he spoke of the black and red danger and, also, dropped the word 'freemason'. The argument was interrupted after a short time when I entered and wished everyone a happy New Year. Hitler stood at the table and cut off a piece of army bread. Next to it he had put a piece of smoked ham. From the look on his face and, from his energetic movements, it was obvious that he was still very excited. So as to introduce a cheerful voice among those assembled, I asked the question, 'Which of you will become Reichschancellor at the next election?' The little dozy one answered immediately, 'It will be Adolf Hitler and I will be Finance Minister!' In the corner someone, whose name escaped me, sat busying himself with writing letters. He looked at me and remarked, 'What that chap Hitler says is rubbish. Whoever thinks chasing Jews from our country would help us? We must have the Jewish investment; without it, we cannot continue to conduct war and, above all, what does he know of German politics? I have been studying for a couple of years and know better. It seems to me better many Jews than one Christian. In our party, we have many Jews who look after their work interests better than Christians.' Adolf Hitler carried on eating his smoked ham silently. All at once, he turned towards the speaker and now the war of words began again. 'Even though I am an Austrian, I know German ways better than you. You can preach your red gospel to Jews and Marxists but at least spare us.' His opponent retorted, 'If you want to be a painter then you have also studied; now you no longer want to be a painter because you are counting on a sergeant's stripe.' Hitler answered, 'Yes, I always think like a socialist, but I am no traitor. I feel German but I am always conscious of my roots. Every respectable person is more or less a socialist, and nationalists and socialists can be bought into line quite well.'

Both became even more intense and it would not have taken much for a fight to break out said one of them to Hitler who was showing 'red' leanings and had stood at the side of his adversary. With my sword between my knees, I sat on a chair laughing at the change in the two politicians and said, 'Just be calm, you are fighting over the Kaiser's beard; in Berlin they will pass laws without you. Above all, we front-line soldiers are politically moulded, we are only temporarily dictated to by Tommy. For myself, I think Hitler's opinion is quite right.'

One man who, up until now, had remained silent said, 'Yes, despatch rider, if we, like you, only associated with counts and barons then we would all be conservative, but we poor proletariat, how will we take advantage of this bloodshed?' Hitler, in the meantime, spoke again and castigated the system of profits of Jewish bankers, mainly in Austria. Then he added that if he were in power he would free the Germanic race from the Jewish parasites and send these race pollutants and people exploiters to Palestine. Hitler's powerfully expressed views were met with strong laughter. Only his verbal opponent, the studious? social democrat, had a resigned look. Hitler moved away and I asked questions of the others, 'What really is Hitler? I am still not clear about the person; one cannot decide whether he is a social democrat or a monarchist.' Messenger Witzgall thought, 'Yes, Hitler is a monarchist in Germany and in Austria a social democrat. Let us say he is a national democrat.'

On my return to the monastery, I busied myself for a long time with Hitler's idea, amazed by his healthy world view and oratory talent. On other days we exchanged words and came back to yesterday's dispute. I got the impression that, in general, I share his political view, but not all Jews are the same. I would have earned most of my money from Jews and would have been able to convince myself that they would have given very much for respectable purposes. On that Hitler replied, 'This hypocritical mawkishness of the Semitic race, as far as poor people are concerned, is only a means to an end. If the merchant has made a 1,000-mark profit then he generally gives 50 pfennigs for the poor, but only if, because of his generous donation, he gets a good name in public as a respectable man. The Jewish capitalist also knows how to take advantage of poverty and if it earns him the reputation of a respectable person.' On that, I said, 'You are right, Hitler, cheerio.'

During the festivities, our regiment sustained few losses but this static warfare, in its nerve-wracking form, demanded victims every day. Not only bits of trench but also the villages near the front line constantly came under fire. We could not count on a breakthrough until early in the year. The position had to be held further and we hoped the warmer time of year would bring a change and see the start of greater action against the enemy. The relations between the fighting troops had somewhat improved. They were regularly relieved and had, while they remained at rest, at least dry accommodation. It was all better organised as far as the current regulations allowed. To many comrades, static warfare became too boring and often I heard, 'If only it started again, we would no longer wonder why we are still here. At this rate, in three years' time, we will be getting our food once again from the goulash pot.'

At the entrance to the monastery I occasionally got into conversation with a young engineer lieutenant. He told me that before the war he was at university studying political science. Also, he was disgruntled with this static warfare. He added, 'I would rather bring my engineers forward into the storm, even if I lost my life as a result, than have to admit how people from my company are shot daily. Just this evening my best sapper was killed by a stray bullet. He was a carpenter by trade and because he had no more relations, my parents sent him letters and parcels. That man would have gone through fire for me. I have a photograph here and a few possessions which he carried with him and I have stored them away to remember him by.'

A number of engineers marched towards us in the direction of the Grand Place. Each one of them had hidden a twig in their helmet [for identification] and they carried their canteens in their hands. The lieutenant immediately recognised it was some of his men who he had sent to the doctor days ago as they were suffering with dysentery. Now they picked out their leader and one of them called out in good Bavarian, 'Jesus, just look, there is our lieutenant' and, at a quick step, they came up to us and they saluted us with a grin on their faces. The lieutenant laughed as he saluted. The lieutenant jokingly enquired about their illness. A broad-shouldered Lower Bavarian offered the lieutenant a drink from his canteen that was the best medicine for stomach ache. The concoction was beer and schnapps. Benefiting, the lieutenant took a hearty swig but remembered the men who were not as well off, they would have to carry out challenging duties this evening. With an inebriated head anything could happen while doing this dangerous work. The Lower Bavarian slapped him on the chest, 'Lieutenant, for you we would go through hell! When it begins, we would like to scrap with Tommy again.' With that he took his pocketknife from its pouch and, executing an upright about turn, he marched off in the direction of the trenches. In the distance we heard them singing once again 'Die Heldenbraut'.

On a misty afternoon in February, I lay on a bale of straw below my horse's haybox and read *The Decline of Troy*. Then Hitler came to me with the order to go immediately to Colonel Betz. I was supposed to pursue a spy, who, at lunchtime, had crept through our section of the front. I got myself ready, put the polished saddle on my horse so that she looked like a racehorse and, at a sharp canter, we went to the staff quarters. Having arrived there, I left my horse in front of the entrance untethered, stroked her neck and said, 'Girl, you must stay here', and like a statue, she stood still. The assembled soldiers were surprised that my horse obeyed my every word. I had to put up with many jokes, among which a question from Adolf Hitler, 'As if your horse can read and write?' I answered him 'Adolf, you will never become as clever as my girl. She has a sixth sense and you only have five.'

Via Sergeant Umann, I reported to Colonel Betz who gave me the details about which direction I should pursue the spy. Probably, he will try to reconnoitre our artillery position. Identification as follows: small stocky figure, black goatee, aquiline nose, wearing supposed Prussian sergeant's uniform and field cap. It was high time because as soon as the spy was able to reach a bigger village, every pursuit would have been in vain. The civil population would have already taken care of his safety. In front of the doors to the house stood my horse again in her best bib and tucker only this time a rope was fixed to the saddle. The orderlies were up to something again, I thought, and hid the rope in my coat pocket. From the horse I peered into the room; someone stood there with a mischievous look and a voice called, 'We have got you a lasso so that you can catch the spy better.' Loud laughter accompanied my riding away. As I left the village I happened upon despatch rider Wind with his quick Prussian horse. Wind was a dashing comrade, a real horseman. He had served actively with the first cavalry regiment. His strong facial features and his healthy complexion made him look rather pleasant. We both stopped and

I asked him to accompany me on the hunt for the spy. 'Have you a rope with you so that we can tie it to the horse's tail?' I reached into my pocket and showed him my lasso.

At a quick gallop we rode across country. Outside Groene Linde we separated and agreed upon three pistol shots in case one of us discovered the spy. After about a quarter of an hour of toing and froing, I heard three pistol shots, the sound coming from quite close by. I called out as, through the thick fog, I could not see more than 10m. Wind answered, he stood on guard on the path. He had the spy. I did not manage to weave myself through the labyrinth of hedges and wire fencing. I really could not see anyone but just heard excited voices. 'You want to be a German officer, you are a spy. If you do anything else, I will shoot you down.' When I reached them both, I noticed immediately that the outward appearance of the arrested man corresponded with the description given. Wind held the revolver to his face, and I explained to him why my comrade was threatening him. The captain became blue and red from anger and cried, 'I am a German officer, you are highwaymen and thieves. Here is my pass and my photograph.' 'We aren't interested, we cannot establish whether the papers are genuine or forged. For now, you are our prisoner.'

We let the captain walk between our horses and he complained to us in the most terrible terms until Wind was deaf to it, and he asked about my rope which I was carrying in the bag. The captain turned round at this in order to see what that meant, then Wind shouted at him, 'You villain, you filthy spy, just look, if you don't co-operate I am going to tie you to my horse and drag you across to the Tommies.' The captain became pale with anger and powerlessness.

Finally, we reached the house of the artillery staff. There I explained the facts of the case, briefly, to a major. He took the captain's papers and moved away. About a quarter of an hour later, the major came and explained that the arrested captain was the leader of a Prussian machine-gun company, and there could be severe consequences for us. I immediately fetched the form from Colonel Betz which listed the identification marks of the spy. He read it and scrutinised the captain again and, in so doing, he could not conceal a furtive laugh. With mixed feelings we set off and reached the edge of Messines in darkness. In good military fashion I was expected to report to Colonel Betz. From his questions I recognised that the arrested captain had already spoken to him on the telephone. He asked me, laughing, whether I had acted according to the Hun system. I answered him, 'If the captain had been the spy, I would have brought him back dead or alive.' I wanted to jump onto my horse which was already hoofing impatiently at the ground. Then one of the orderlies called me back and Colonel Betz, smiling, pushed some cigars into my hand.

For my comrades, these stories were a welcome opportunity to ridicule me good and proper. Adolf Hitler, with his gift of the gab, had contributed the most and, at the time, had hung the lasso on the saddle. Today, I no longer want to claim that he was not completely innocent.

After four months of static warfare on the bend of the Ypres Canal, we were finally supposed to be relieved and transferred to rest in reserve at Roubaix/Tourcoing. The trenches had, because of so much rain, transformed into streams in which, during the cold winter days and nights, soldiers had to stop under the heaviest fire. It is impossible to describe all the sad scenes which had played out during these months. Only the little wooden crosses on the bend of the Ypres were silent witnesses to the fighting.

On the night of 9 March, our regiment set out to march towards Tourcoing. Shortly before Comines, I rode ahead to quickly say goodbye to the people I had been quartered with. Madame Culier carefully hid a sandwich in my pocket. Madeleine gave me a picture of herself and as I remounted, Mr Culier said adieu as ahead the regiment was passing the entrance to the village. It was 3 o'clock in the morning and bitterly cold. The messengers rode ahead of 3rd battalion. I leant back to my comrade Wind and, after a while, he said to me, 'If my dream is correct, we are shortly in for something bad. Tonight, before marching off, I had laid down under the haybox and gone to sleep. In my dream I was riding along a street on which I encountered many ambulance wagons full of wounded. Batteries galloped crazily past me. You will see our calm will not last long.' I replied, 'Hans, don't look so down, we are going to enjoy ourselves today in Roubaix.' He shook his head, 'I have seen many dead comrades and have the feeling that today we will see that again.' Now I became angry, but should I not remain positive? 'Our reserve division will never be used in a counterattack, we have, only today, been taken out of the line and, after this long march, we are going to get our rest.' Wind turned his horse around and rode along the column to his battalion.

At the break of day, we made a stop in a village and the field canteen distributed coffee to the troops. It had got colder and most had not slept for two days and were extremely frozen. The strong 'real' coffee with rum put the troops in a better mood. I rode along the marching column to meet some comrades who I knew from our days back in the regiment in Munich. I found few of them; many had fallen or had gone home wounded. Around the munitions wagon stood the regimental orderlies drinking their coffee from the top of a kettle. For the first time I saw that the last few months of static warfare had not passed without leaving its mark on Hitler. It had caught up with him. I said, 'Because you are all still here we shall have a good time in Tourcoing.' Some laughed, some remained serious and did not trust my 'Fata Morgana'. Towards midday we reached our destination and we despatch riders found good accommodation in a brewery. Having fed our horses and got the stabling in order, we took the tram to Roubaix. There we bought the necessary toiletries, wrote some field postcards, and hoped to meet up later in a cafe at the station.

This morning's conversation with my comrade Wind happened to come to mind and, as no one was advised of our prohibited trip, I sent the messenger Kellner back into our quarters so that should anything happen, he would advise us immediately. In the cafe, we found a pair of beautiful blonde Flemish girls who immediately approached us amicably and made food for us served with wine and French schnapps. Naturally, we lacked for nothing. Each of us wanted to show our affection and soon we were in the most joyous mood.

My comrade Wind sat next to me, the blonde Flemish girl pressing up against him firmly. I made him aware of his dream, 'You see blonde girls and no wounded soldiers!' He answered angrily, 'Just wait, it's not yet evening.' The little blonde pressed herself more firmly on the handsome horseman with the flattering words, 'To your health darling, I love you with all my heart.' My dear Wind had forgotten all his dreams and found himself in seventh heaven. The latter blissful moment was interrupted with a blow. The doors were flung open. Kellner crashed in and reported that the regiment was already marching on Neuve-Chapelle where the

English had broken through the German positions. We were evacuating. He had already saddled our horses in the quarters.

Comrade Wind shouted, 'That's a mess.' The little blonde still hung tightly around him and did not want to let him go until I explained in her mother tongue why we had to leave quickly. She began to cry and, in her sorrow, wished the English the worst. We ran as quickly as we could to the tram stop and, when the wagon came, I jumped immediately up to the conductor who I ordered to travel through to Tourcoing. Initially he refused, but when I pressed 10 francs into his hand, he agreed. In double-quick time we got back to our quarters. Quickly we were in the saddle and, at the fastest gallop, got to the station. From the bridge, which crossed the freight depot, we saw the last transport of our regiment leaving. It was only us stood there! Immediately, I asked a civilian for the shortest route to Neuve-Chapelle and how many kilometres it was.

I quickly checked the accuracy of what he said on the map and we rode as quickly as possible along the Ypres Canal. This route which the freight ships had been transported up and down had a bridle path alongside and we could ride at the quickest gallop on this. My brave horse had to breathe deeply in order for us to reach our destination quickly. She went like a machine under me. Only with great trouble could Wind keep pace with me on his Prussian horse. The remaining despatch riders had heavier horses and, as a result, remained, despite constant spurring on, behind us. From time to time we had to ride at a trot so that the animals could have a breather. This slowing down became tiresome to me. I overtook despatch rider Wind and rode on quickly with my horse.

Halfway to Torn, we encountered two wounded from a Prussian infantry regiment. They told us that they had been attacked by numerous English battalions and behind them further powerful cavalry formations stood ready to attack, in order to roll up the German front and eventually break through. As a consequence of this great superiority, the regiment had to fall back and Neuve-Chapelle had fallen into English hands. Thank goodness Bavarian divisions were on their way to Torn and would probably, this evening, make a counterattack. When I told them that the sixth Bavarian reserve division, to which I also belonged, had been put on alert in Roubaix several hours ago, one of them said, 'Then the Tommies are going to get their thrashing, for they are more afraid of you Bavarians than us Prussians, we are glad to have got out of the mess.' Wishing them a speedy recovery, I rode on to Torn.

Quite close, I heard the dull roar of cannons; shell explosions accompanied me on my way. On a street not far from the canal, a column of Red Cross wagons was moving and past them galloped the munitions column to the battery. At times the artillery fire was so violent that it was a single muffled rumble, and you could only detect the heavy shells.

Just outside Torn I asked civilians for the quickest way to the station. Their disturbed faces showed great fear; should they stay or should they flee. A heavily pregnant woman with a child in her arms cried heartbreakingly. I assured them that they need have no fear and could stay here peacefully, we would not let the English through. Out of joy at of my positive news, a small elderly lady bought me a cup of coffee and cared for my horse.

With the greatest difficulty I was able to get through to the station. An endless column of vehicles was moving on the main road to La Bassée. Reserve batteries galloped past me. Artillery men sat, like statues with serious faces, on their ammunition cases. In the meantime, machine-gun sections pushed through; on the right and left of the road infantry columns had lined up and were in the process of marching to the front.

Night had already fallen when I reached the station. Cavalrymen stood there armed with rifles and hand grenades ready to march in order to support the infantry regiments. However, I saw none of my comrades. An officer referred me to the marshalling yard from where the Bavarians had marched off to the front half an hour ago. I could meet them at Aubers. At the camps in the freight depot stood our unloaded munitions with the subdued field canteen. Stopping a junior officer, I asked after the regimental staff, but he could not give me any information. Behind me I heard a voice, 'Hello despatch rider, how did you get so quickly to Torn? Just now, Colonel Betz asked after you.' It was Sergeant Steger, who was now illuminating my face with a pocket lantern. I told him of the unauthorised trip from Tourcoing to Roubaix. He laughed and gave me exact stopping points where I could find the regimental staff. Looking back at my horse, which was very worn out after the fast ride, I mounted and took a couple of litres of oats from Sergeant Steger. I had a quick snack, but it did not taste good to me because the worry of my absence from the regiment left me restless.

Now I took the things back to the regimental staff. As the other despatch riders moved in their horses were gleaming with sweat. Briefly I gave them information and sent them to the munitions where Sergeant Steger gave them further instruction so they could find their battalions.

The avenue of poplars along Neuve-Chapelle street had been knocked down in the afternoon by the shelling. Carefully the way had to be cleared. The fire on the street lasted all night because the English knew exactly that the German reserves had moved in. On one of the crossroads lay a shot-up ammunition truck on which a horse's innards hung. The other's neck had been torn out. They had to be removed by a passing ammunitions column. The direct hit had totally smashed the ammunition truck. One could not confirm how many drivers had died but, judging by the helmets and remains lying around, it must have been many. The drivers worked with utter disgust and had, at this dangerous spot, at any moment, to expect the same fate themselves. With one of my hands, I held my horse, illuminating her with a fading lantern held in the other. The air was full of the smell of sulphur which the wind blew over. The sky was coloured red from the burning villages.

I passed a small forest which ran along the road. Behind a statue of the mother of god, I dismounted and got my bearings on the map. At that moment a battery began to fire close by and I heard an order. Shortly I rode, determinedly, away from the forest where the shots had been fired. Behind a thick bush a battery had taken position and was in the process of getting the range. The drivers stood by their still harnessed horses. To the lieutenant who was directing the firing I asked about the regimental staff and he showed me Aubers Farm on the map where he was currently quartered.

The wind blew the smoke from the burning shot-up houses into my face. At a burning farm in Aubers I jumped down from my horse. Field telephonists were again mending telephone wires shot up by the shelling. Having got information from the telephonists, I found I was only a short distance away from our regimental staff. There I reported immediately to Colonel Betz. He stood at a table in the parlour of the farmhouse, bent over the map and was very serious. The regimental orderlies were stopped there in so far as they were not going into the yard taking messages.

The enemy fire raged incessantly, only weakening in short intervals. A non-commissioned officer who was with Colonel Betz in the living room called through the glassless window to a messenger. With that he called out various names, among them that of Adolf Hitler, but the majority of the orderlies had already been sent away. One came to the window. Adolf Hitler was supposed to be on the way to the first battalion with a message but probably he had not got through, he himself had just turned back from the front, his way literally ringed with shells. For five months he had been working as a messenger, but he had never made his way through such a strong bombardment. Messenger Dammerl interjected, 'Don't worry about Hitler, he will soon come through and, if he has to, he will creep into a ditch like a cat.' Owing to the terrible explosions, part of the roof of Colonel Betz's room had been ripped off. The windowpanes fell out of their frames; these were nerve-wracking hours. We spoke only when necessary, duties was carried out mechanically.

In the wider vicinity of the farm, the noise settled down. I was amazed that our farm had been spared. As I momentarily had no order to carry out, I bought my horse under the cover of a stable. I lay down in the pig pen and requested a messenger to call me if I had to ride away. Because of tiredness I fell asleep straightaway, but a terrible explosion nearby soon woke me. I positively tore out of the camp. My next thought concerned my brave 'girl'; she had torn up the rein by which she was tethered and was running terrified around the stable. It was already 5 o'clock in the morning, thank goodness the night would soon be over!

In order not to be buried alive with my horse in the eventual shelling of the farm, I fetched her from the stable and stayed out in the open. Colonel Betz was busy in the parlour studying the map. His adjutant stood next to him and the telephonist gave the orders on to battalion staffs through his apparatus. I tethered my horse on a lawn in the garden, and, out of curiosity, set out on the way to Aubers. The church was shot up, inside lay a great pile of bricks and mortar, the roof was broken, only the walls still stood partially.

Outside a house in which the dressing station was situated, many orderlies carried wounded who should have been transported back by

Red Cross wagons. Some ambulances stood ready to take away the dead. Steaming field canteens were preparing food, for many their last meal. From the dressing station came two orderlies with a freshly dressed, badly wounded man, and wanted to have him transported back in the ambulance; when the latter had been loaded, they buttoned the canvas cape on him a second time and wanted to lay him on the stretcher. During this short time, I stood with the heavily wounded man, the blood flowing continually from his mouth. He looked at me with starry eyes, his pupils wide. When I cleaned his mouth with my handkerchief, he made a movement as if he wanted to sit up and the orderly said to his comrade, 'He's already dead.'

Inside the house two doctors dressed the wounded. Although I had smelled much blood and had often seen death, I could not bear the scene in this room. The air in the room was choking. One man whose leg had been shot off winked at me. It would have been bad for me if I had not left quickly. Behind the house lay dead English men, still quite young people. The locks of a young Irish man hung matted with blood over his still-rosy face. It almost gave the impression that he was asleep. The cemetery at Aubers resembled a large field of craters. Limbs of the dead lay resting there as if scattered by the wind. Dead English and Germans were in rows next to each other, many soldiers busied themselves digging mass graves which they soaked with white lime.

I heard shots exploding over me incessantly. German anti-aircraft guns shot at English pilots who moved over our position like buzzards circling. For a long time I had not wanted to be far from the regimental staff's quarters and returned again.

At the church I met Adolf Hitler, he was going again with an order to the firing position, flexible and unconcerned as always. On some occasions I had observed that when he was sent with an order to the trenches, he never missed looking at the map just to work out which points might be dangerous for him on the way. He knew shrewdly to go around these points and, with prudence and bravery, he always reached his destination.

I would never want to lessen the achievements of the remaining regimental messengers, they always gave their best, but Hitler was, however, superior to them because not only is bravery demanded of a good messenger, but above all intelligence and astuteness. Also, at the regimental staff they knew this well. On those occasions that I heard Colonel Betz need a reliable man for an important message, Hitler's name was called.

At the order of Colonel Betz, I was supposed to take a message to a member of staff in our division. A field telephonist, who was making coffee between two bricks in the farmyard, allowed me to fill up my field cup and then I fed my 'girl' and made her ready to leave. In the meantime, messenger Dammerl came over and got himself some coffee too. Sitting side by side he told me of his latest message errand. 'If today one of us is sent forward to the front, he won't come back again as the firing is terrible. If I get it today, I hope that I don't have to suffer too long.' I said to him, 'I have already seen Hitler sent up again to the front but don't think he will get it.' 'Yes', reflected Dammerl, 'Hitler carries just his message bag which, one day will be unfastened, but he must be careful that he doesn't have to give up his life for it.'

A regimental orderly came out of the farm bringing the remaining messages, and we went our separate ways with a 'cheerio'. The artillery fire again raged with undiminished intensity. Our artillery, which had been put in during the night, had now adjusted itself and begun to fire.

Burst of Fire at Neuve Chapelle

Today I saw Adolf Hitler again, pacing round restlessly like a tiger, at the farm in Halpegarbe. He could not wait to be despatched by Colonel Betz with a message. Even the colonel himself said, 'I don't believe that my orderlies will get through this bombardment.'

All contact was, at that time, broken between the battalions, and the orderlies had the difficult task of re-establishing this to some extent. We had no further contact with the regiment and I recall Colonel Betz sitting at the map in Halpegarbe, striking the table with anger, 'How can I give orders if I don't know where my men are?'

The confusion had come about because the various formations of our units, when they were unloaded in the Don, were marched off to the front and, on their own initiative, got mixed up in the fight between Prussian troops. The orderlies Hitler, Wimmer, Lippert, Schmidt and Weiss had the task of re-establishing contact as soon as possible, but this was made very difficult by the dreadful shelling and the sodden ground. Hitler explained later, in Fournes, that on his message trips he was covered by enemy fire and that he could only move forward by crawling from one shell hole to another; sometimes he could not see more than 10m ahead of him because of the sulphur fumes. During the night, the English had brought up lots of artillery so that they were superior to us in the number of shells as well as troops. When I mounted, shells exploded in our farm, and my frightened horse did not want to stand still. During the night, she had become really nervous. Raging machine-gun fire accompanied me on the way and got noticeably stronger. Despite the message having three crosses, I stopped my horse and looked at the hellish drama. The land was shrouded in smoke and sulphur fumes. In the air there was a constant flashing of exploding shrapnel, and you could only distinguish masses of earth flung as high as a house from the exploding shells. Initially, I did not know where I was, as the enemy once again put the whole road that led to Neuve-Chapelle under fire. It was evident to me that this was an English advance.

It was high time I gained free ground. I chased across country from the road which leads from the Don to La Bassée, the machine-gun fire had diminished and now you could only make out a little machine-gun fire with its regular tack-tack. Above the infantry positions, yellow and black clouds moved and instinctively I thought of my comrades who lay outside. I recalled the images of this morning, the dying at the church in Aubers, Hitler as he went to the front, messenger Dammerl's melancholic look. I was struck by a revulsion at this mass murder.

I got my bearings on the map and looked for the farm I had to take the message to. Then a powerful salvo struck a column of transport on the La Bassée road. The hideous cries of the horses and wounded rang in my ears. One part of the column was shrouded in smoke; I recognised the drivers only from their helmets and saw them retreat in order to fetch help.

I could not stop any longer and set off on my way to Herlies, in whose vicinity the artillery staff was. The path led through the firing range but was significantly shorter than shown on the map via Salomé. On one side of the street there were farms and I tried to water my thirsty horse. Through the arch-shaped farm gate, I saw an old man in clogs with a whistle in his mouth. He watched the gleaming wooden balcony of his house and constantly spat in the fire. The barn was completely, and the house partly, burnt out. Only a few rooms remained in reasonable condition from what I could see through the paneless windows from my horse. The old man came up to me, greeted me and shoved a piece of chewing tobacco in his mouth. In answer to my question whether I could water my horse, he shook his head. 'There is still water in the well, but it is no longer drinkable. The soldiers have thrown in all their filth but for your beautiful horse I will fetch some from the cistern.' I dismounted to examine the farm more closely. The old man came out again and brought me water which my thirsty horse drank quickly. The old man told me that, in 1870, he had ridden at the big attack at Reichshofen. He was wounded at that time, imprisoned and, until the peace of Magdeburg, he had worked for a gardener. 'Why do you remain alone in this shot-up farm?' 'I would like to die here. My poor dog is already dead.' He went back into the living room and brought out a dead pinscher in a basket that had been killed by the shelling. With a 'Good day, sir', I rode out of the gate. Turning around again, I saw him waving with his cap under the archway.

Half an hour later I gave in my order at the farm. An artillery major got one of his people to give me something to eat, my horse got a portion of oats and, after a short stay, I set out for home. Behind a hedge, northwest of Herlies, some Prussian batteries were firing. Whole rows of shells lay behind the guns which were covered with cut hedge branches. When I came up to it the battery took a short break. The artillerymen sat with yellow faces on the gun carriages fortified by their mess tins and made jokes. I asked whether the English or the Germans had attacked. A bombardier informed me that, half an hour ago, the English had, again, put in an offensive against the 16th and 17th Bavarian regiments. In response to my comments that I was a messenger for one of these regiments, the bombardier grimaced, 'What, and you are still alive? You have had some luck there. Most of your regiment will not come back again.'

Concerned, I rode off again and, close to Aubers, I saw messenger Wimmer; he realised that I wanted to ride to the farm and called over to me, 'The farm is surrounded. Colonel Betz has gone to the battalions at the front. However, you can ride back to the supply depot. Colonel Betz has sent all the messengers back there and ordered them to stay there and, only when Mend comes back, should he report to the Regimental Doctor Rühl who is at the regimental dressing station in Aubers.' Now I wanted to know whether anything had happened to any of my friends, but he knew nothing, only that he had seen Schmidt and Hitler around midday.

I stopped at one of the houses that had been spared by the shelling, and led my horse into the living room which, before my arrival, appeared to have served as a stable. Here I could calmly settle my horse and shortly afterwards take off the saddle. It began to get dark and I lay wearily on a bale of straw, but rest was unthinkable. The lice in the straw were uncomfortable. In the dark I put the saddle on the horse again to seek different quarters for the night, preferring to be exposed to shellfire than lice. I was hardly on my horse when the shelling of Aubers began. I was concerned, in my anger, not to stay around and rode to the church square. There stood, again in rows, the ambulances and lightly wounded men wandered in makeshift bandages on foot back to the Don if they had not had the chance to catch a vehicle. From behind the canvas sheets of the closed wagons, one heard the groaning of the seriously wounded. Soon I found Dir, a captain in the medical corps who, along with a junior doctor, had his hands full. He applied the first bandages and made such comical remarks that many, despite their pain, laughed out loud. Dir, whether he was under fire or behind the front lines, was always calm and when, sometimes, shells exploded nearby and fear showed in the eyes of the orderlies, he remained completely relaxed and, with the help of a coarse joke, helped everyone through the dangerous situation. Adolf Hitler could, at best, reproduce his strength of expression.

When I asked Dir whether he still needed assistance, he turned to me, 'At the moment no, but can you get me a few good cigars? What is best for now are the powers with which I am operating.' I gave him some and hid one away for myself.

'So, you are right, stay with your mounts now until I need you later but take care that you remain close by. Don't go looking for girls.'

Towards midnight more wounded and dead were brought up, the doctors were struggling to cope. In the main street, at the blacksmith's, the heaviest calibre shells exploded in salvos and we did not feel very safe at the dressing station. I could have found a quieter place but, in these dangerous circumstances, I kept an eye on my comrades and gravitated to those who seemed worn out. Towards 2 in the morning, on the third day of battle, an orderly came with a message for Dr Rühl. In front of the house, he told me about the regiment's situation in more detail.

At 4 o'clock the fighting gradually abated. Only a muffled rumbling could be heard coming from Neuve-Chapelle.

After the first success of the English, where a piece of ground at Neuve-Chapelle had fallen into their hands, they could make no further incursion on our division. At daybreak Dr Rühl sent me with a message to Don. I did not need to return again as he had been informed of the withdrawal of our division. After taking my order over, I was to look for the supply depot and its orderlies who were stationed there with the horses to send them to the dressing station at Aubers. In Salomé I found the crew, most of whom knew me. 'Hello horseman, you are still alive! We thought that you had been shot down from your billy goat!' Vice Sergeant Witzgall, who had been released from the regiment, thought that we would no longer go to Roubaix and would probably be put in near Neuve-Chapelle. In the meantime, I met yet more comrades; they were all pleased that an old member of the List regiment had proved his worth again and again. Each one was proud of the good reputation of the regiment, and every comrade who was there from the start let incoming replacements feel the spirit of the List regiment very keenly. I had often met troops from other regiments but with no other unit was the regimental pride as marked as with us.

On the railway line from Don to La Bassée stood a little railwayman's cottage which was not occupied. I wanted to use this as my quarters for the night and informed the quartermaster. While I was feeding my horse, other messengers rode up. These were comrades Langwieder, Loibl, Höntsch, Wind and the Kellner brothers.

When I wanted to move my quarters into the little railwayman's cottage, I found the shutters closed and heard through the window the Ave Maria being said and, in between, 'God Bless France'. At my knocking and calling, the door was not opened until I threatened in French that, if it was not opened voluntarily, I would break in. The next moment the door was opened by an old lady with rosary beads and a prayer book in her hand. In tears, she asked whether I was an Alsatian or a spy because I spoke French. 'I am neither Alsatian nor spy but a messenger from a regiment over there.'

Pointing at my blue and white insignia, she asked me, 'You are Bavarian and a Catholic aren't you?' Agreeing with everything, although I am a Protestant, and, with a eulogy on Catholic Bavaria, she turned away from me in order to fetch coffee and bacon from a grocer's for my evening meal. Eagerly she soon returned from the village and advised me to leave immediately as the English were arriving today.

In the village street I had seen many German troops coming back from the front. For their safety they wanted to sleep in Salomé in a friend's cellar tonight. I tried to convince the old lady that the gossip of the inhabitants was not true; we had won the battle of Neuve-Chapelle and the troops, which I had seen, had pulled back from the front on a German order because the enemy made no further attack. She was now calm again, gave me my supper and, a short time later, I laid down to sleep.

During the night, our division was relieved and collected behind the front. When I went to the supply depot the following morning, most of the companies of our regiment were there, and lay or stood in groups around the field canteen. An armourer wanted to hold a roll call, but it took quite a while for the exhausted soldiers to assemble. It was evident from their tense faces that the hard fighting had profoundly affected them. Many lay in deep sleep and, shaken up, went without food despite their hunger so as not to be disturbed from their rest.

I just had time to learn the details about the fighting as I went from one group to another, kicking some comrades who had laid down between munitions wagons. These were regimental messengers, among them Adolf Hitler. A few batmen stood by writing field postcards or reading their letters from home.

Some rested on their stomachs using their knapsacks to protect their heads and gave the impression that they were dead. Hitler had rested his billycan on the wheel of a munitions wagon and turned around as I passed him. He gave me with a piercing look as if he wanted to say, 'Where have you been loitering during the fighting?' Compared with his completely exhausted comrades, he seemed relatively fresh, just as earlier in Messines where his outward appearance didn't given anything away and he was always ready to go. His borrowed uniform, which was too big for him, was covered in dirt and shell sulphur and bore witness to the fact that yesterday he had been heavily involved.

But whoever concerned themselves with Hitler at that time, although he was just a messenger like all others, one noticed a certain superiority in him without him making anything of it. He carried what was he ordered to with great care and accuracy.

Looking around I saw an acquaintance who knew where to find the orderlies. I headed towards the messengers' wagon. Seeing Hitler, I said, 'The Austrian, of course, has no time to sit back and do nothing; if he is not here, we carry on as if we have lost the war but he comes through everywhere. He is as cunning as a fox and knows exactly when it's time to leave.' The day before yesterday, during a barrage on the front, I saw him running, paying full attention to the task in hand! If he was the son of a banker, he wouldn't have to wait as long to become a lieutenant but as an Austrian in the List regiment, he can't count on anything at all especially when they hear that he is not good at speaking to the Hapsburgs. The non-commissioned officer was a quiet but brave comrade; despite this he was always overlooked with promotions and decorations so that he often felt marked down. The regiment remained for a few days' rest, the companies were organised again and occasional roll calls held. According to the opinion of the battalion commander at that time, the regiment had, during the 3-day battle, counted 500 to 600 dead and wounded. In the few days of rest, we organised our equipment; we messengers cared for our horses, saddles and shoeing.

In my quarters we had a happy time in the evening. Here, for the moment, we did not fear exploding shells. The cottage lay to one side of the village less in range than Salomé. Messengers and good friends came due to the atmosphere in my idyllic quarters and with strong coffee, cigarettes and a requisitioned bottle of red wine, we passed many joyful hours. Everything sad was forgotten. The old lady just shook her head because we were able to laugh after such an intense battle. She kept praising us with the words, 'Gentlemen, you are brave soldiers, you have courage for France.'

After three days' rest, we were put into a section of the front at Fromelles. That was an unpleasant surprise for the troops who hoped to go Roubaix to rest. Before I left my quarters two Landsturm infantrymen with heavily stuffed rucksacks came and took them over. They gave the lady coffee, sausage and further provisions for which she said a thousand times 'Thank you, sir.' I climbed on my horse, looked out of the stalls and rode off shortly afterwards with the lieutenant, the first of the regiment to reach Fournes to find quarters.

On 17 March 1915 when I rode through the streets of Fournes for the first time, I considered that I had stayed in this village for longer than a year. Apart from some houses which had been shot up during the capture of 1914, Fournes was in comparatively good condition. The better families had fled in October 1914. Only the mayor, a brewery owner who had studied at the brewery school at Weihenstephan and spoke good German, and working families remained.

In the middle of the village in a former girls' boarding school the area commander was accommodated. On the edge of the village in the direction of Fromelles our regimental staff had taken over a beautiful private house as their quarters. The battalion staff had been allocated the largest private buildings, the companies the school halls and all bigger rooms. Outside the village in the direction of Illies an avenue lined with poplar trees branched off to the Chateau du compte d'Hespel, in which the brigade commander had taken up residence. From the Place du Pavilion, the route was about halfway from Fromelles to the combat zone. On our arrival suitable accommodation for men and horses was sought.

Dr Dir was quartered in a blacksmith's shop. The blacksmith had fled; only the first floor was inhabited by a lady and her daughter, who was pretty as a picture. I had heard that she had already had a non-commissioned officer quartered there and, as she had been a teacher in civilian life and that her daughter was also a teacher, they had both understood very well what was required of them. After seeing the room, we arranged that Dr Dir would have his quarters here. The ladies requested that I also stay there. I looked clean and healthy and they were afraid of men from the trenches bringing lice into their rooms. I promised and wrote on the door 'occupied by the doctor of the 16th infantry regiment'.

Now I still had to find a stable for my 'girl'. I wanted to have her near me, because, at that time, horses were frequently stolen by people from different units. I found a former goat's stable which was slightly too small, but my good horse was already used to such accommodation. Having returned to the blacksmith's, I encountered an artillery man on the step with a new, grey officer's trunk. His lieutenant had his quarters here and I was not to go up. It made me angry. I asked whether the lieutenant was young or old, upon which he told me that he had only come from Germany with him today and that he was no older than 19.

In my anger I went upstairs and saw new saddlebags and also a coat outside the room. I called the madame. Immediately doors were flung open and a fresh-faced boy appeared. 'Are you the corporal who wants to have his quarters here? Make sure you don't come any closer.' He was so rude to me that I grabbed my sword and approached him aggressively. He was small and moved back into his room and bolted the door. I was still not satisfied and went to look for Dr Dir, who immediately went with me into the blacksmith's and summoned the lieutenant via the lady. Somewhat dejected, she stepped out of the room and, in the sharpest manner, told the lieutenant that he had immediately to leave his quarters. He still wanted to complain about my behaviour, but quickly appreciated that he had no idea of the spirit of a front-line soldier. When I came back again in the evening, the lieutenant had departed.

On the edge of Fournes, Colonel Betz had, with his staff, quartered Regimental Sergeant Umann and his orderlies. The distinguished buildings in the Place du Pavilion were extraordinarily spacious and suitable for the regimental staff. In the back building, in which the kitchen was set up, lay the regimental chancellery and the orderlies. The house servants had stayed while the owners had long since fled.

On the afternoon of the second day in Fournes, I was ordered by the brigade commander Kiefhaber to the castle. The ground around the entrance to the village was shot up and thoughts came to me about our, supposedly, safe accommodation. Riding through a short avenue of poplars I saw the castle lying in front of me. I handed over my message and looked at the park which also housed a smallish zoo. However, at this time, the only inhabitants were big rats. Around the building was a moat with a small bridge which, just then, a man was crossing with an axe on his back, and he greeted me in a friendly way. It was the steward who had given twenty-five years' service. His master had fled, he said, but he had received the order to remain in the castle until the war was over, which amounted to a death sentence because the shelling could no longer be stopped. Yesterday, English pilots had got their bearings above the whole area. I calmed him. 'Don't be afraid, sir, we have been in the villages up until now, have been shot up and, as you see, I am still alive.'

At the entrance to the village a well-known sergeant asked me where I was quartered. 'What, in the blacksmith's? You are really sitting in a hot spot there. Two roads cross there. If I were you, I would look for different quarters.' Outside the house of the regimental staff, Colonel Betz asked after my horse and how I'd got out of Neuve-Chapelle. I received an order from him to go to Houbordin and looked for the orderlies in the back building where I received a great welcome. In the corner stood Adolf Hitler who was engrossed in a book. He wore the service cross. Aside from that, there was nothing else worthy of note.

Next day I was taken to task by an artillery captain because of the clash with the young lieutenant. The captain could well understand my behaviour toward the lieutenant, however, the captain, who kept a pair of much-loved hens, and for whom he had found no accommodation, had asked me for these quarters. After a discussion with Dr Dir he got it, but after two days the first English greeting exploded nearby and shrouded the whole house in smoke and fumes, so that I was already thinking of the end of the captain and those who had quartered him.

In the days following I saw him looking out of the window pensively. Then, however, fate took over, he was wounded and the hens, his darlings, flew with the shed into the air. Both the French girls were, luckily for them, not present during the bombardment. Now we were glad we had changed our accommodation.

Outside, in the early days, at intervals the western and eastern exits from Fournes were shot up where we lay; the remainder of the village was spared the bombardment. All the same, the threat remained like a grumbling volcano.

Front Line at Fromelles

While we lay at rest here we heard from the front at Fromelles, where our regiment could be put in any day. The air pressure of the heavy shell explosions caused windowpanes to rattle continuously and the ceilings in rooms fell in. Our laughing and joking was, to a great extent, gallows humour which was required to get us through the uncertain time of waiting. It gave us something different to think about. The front line at Fromelles had already claimed enough victims, as proven by the many wooden crosses in the newly acquired cemetery. From now on we had the honour of increasing them.

When I rode, for the first time, at darkness to Fromelles, halfway behind the farm at La Varines rifle bullets whistled around my ears. Fromelles lay entirely shot to pieces. Only a cross standing in the centre remained untouched, the post standing out in front providing protection; it was viewed by the soldiers as a miracle. When I arrived at the cellars of the regimental staff's house, Adolf Hitler stood up and said to me that he had to go to the trenches with a message. The first path to a new position is always the hardest because one does not know how things stand. I said, 'You are a mole, you always come through, don't let them shoot you in the stomach!' With the words, 'That's my worry, my dear Mend', he withdrew.

As I had often heard from other messengers, the lousy, most forward positions did not afford much protection. They were not deep enough and at the opening shots there had already been many wounded from my battalion. Along this dangerous path Adolf Hitler passed many times daily and, if he wanted to come through safely, had to crawl more than march. The slightest movement did not elude the English sharpshooters.

In the early days of our stay, I often had to bring messages from Fournes to Fromelles and back. On the way there, almost always, comrades approached me. In beautiful weather they sat in trenches in the street and still smoked a cigarette, for on the way from Fromelles to the trench every informality ceased and it opened your eyes to the reality of the situation.

On the fourth day I got a message for Colonel Betz who had his dugout in Fromelles. It had to be delivered quickly. On this morning I had ridden the horse of Lieutenant Weissgerber, a well-known Munich artist.

During the long pause, he could do nothing more with the animal and asked me if I could train it. The horse was East Prussian but headstrong and very nervous; I, therefore, had my misgivings riding with the nervous bay to Fromelles. There was no more time to re-saddle, so I rode off with my pupil. Behind Rosewood Farm, two heavies exploded and my bay almost reared up with fear and terror. Now I held it more firmly between my legs and rode on at a fast gallop. Suddenly I heard a rustling and whistling behind me; looking back I saw a pack of big rats following me. These horrible creatures almost hung on my horse's hooves. I observed the race, as soon as the bay sped up, the rats followed quivering. Finally, this entourage became onerous to me and I rode on at a gallop and they couldn't keep up.

At Lavarie Farm a Bavarian battery with French guns was firing a salvo. My bay reared up in terror and came down with its left hoof between two spokes of a wagon. I immediately tried to free the hoof which sat wedged between the wheel spokes, but every effort was in vain. Finally, an artilleryman had to saw through a spoke in order to release the hoof.

Behind the houses in Lavarie I overtook Adolf Hitler and messenger Schmidt. They were amazed that I was not riding my horse and cracked jokes. In his humorous manner, Hitler bowed before me like a master of ceremonies in front of His Majesty. In order to put an end to his wind-up, I gave the spur to my horse which reared up and would have hit Hitler with its front legs if the latter had not been as nimble as a greyhound jumping across the trenches. Finally, again they wanted to know why I wasn't riding my horse. 'I must leave her in Fournes for a few days until she is dry because yesterday I blackened her in case I have to be at your funeral procession.' With a 'cheerio' we separated, and in a few minutes I had given my message to the staff in Fromelles. While I waited for an answer, enemy shells exploded incessantly in Fromelles. Now Hitler and Schmidt arrived. They did not stay long but set off straight away on their way to the trenches. In passing, Hitler shouted, picking up his helmet, 'Goodbye Cavalry Captain!' And I shouted back, 'Be gone or I will throw a shovel of dirt at you.'

I had hardly left the regimental staff headquarters when I saw the little black, yellow clouds hovering. It was not scary to my bay, he wanted to move off at a trot and only with much effort could I stop him. Immediately behind Lavarie, where the rats had accompanied me, a shell flew away over me and exploded at Rosewood Farm. I saw a person fly into the air and as I was close by I rode over at a gallop in order to check. A poplar had been torn out of the earth, next to it lay an infantryman so covered with earth that only his rucksack, a foot and his rifle hanging over his back were to be seen. As one of his legs twitched, I jumped off, let my horse run and freed him from the earth and unbuttoned his jacket. Unfortunately, he was beyond help; the poor chap had a serious stomach wound, his entrails were hanging out and his lips were bloodless. Every minute I waited for the release of death for him. Artillerymen who were quartered in the Rosewood Farm had also seen him blown sky high and brought him to Fournes on a strip of canvas where, shortly afterwards, he died.

When I arrived on foot in Fournes, many soldiers were standing on the street and one of them was holding my horse. They thought that its rider must have been wounded. I gave the bay to the batman of Lieutenant Weissgerber.

After the first relief, most of our people who lay in Fromelles and in the trenches were of the opinion that, at the first sign of warm spring weather, the English would intensify their attacks. Until now, they had limited their artillery bombardment just to probing which signified the prelude for what was coming.

Many days in March were spent resting which was only broken by the odd rifle shot, and when I rode to the front line, I often saw groups of soldiers sitting together, playing cards, in the warm spring sunshine. Next to them was a billycan full of coffee, the inevitable worry breaker.

The staff in the battery in Lavarie, mostly the old salts among the artillerymen, made themselves comfortable. They did everything possible during the lull, often economising for eight days on munitions. Some wrote greetings from the Bavarian Landwehr to the English on the shells that stood ready in the shell baskets. Their dugout was furnished with pictures; in the corner stood a divan and tiled stove. Against the wooden wall, on a small table, a dud of considerable capacity was on show. For this reason, at the entrance to their dugout was written in big letters 'TO THE DUD'.

The strength of the battery was its leader, a first lieutenant. He was hugely popular with his men with whom I often saw him playing cards and who just called him 'Handsome Roland'. On a quiet, sunny afternoon while I rode past the artillerymen the first lieutenant allowed me to call in at the 'Villa Dud'. Before I could stand to attention in front of him, he waved it away and passed me a cigar. With his boots off, he lay on the sofa, which looked very much the worse for wear, and invited me to take a seat next to him. Aha, I thought to myself, 'Handsome Roland' wants to talk. He knew that I was a messenger from the List regiment and his artillerymen had already told a lot about me because they had known me since October 1914 as the 'Ghost Rider'. We talked about women and horses and about our active service. With that, he poured me a glass of red wine, then one after another so that I soon could no longer differentiate who was the first lieutenant and who was the corporal, which greatly amused him. We were so cheerful that artillerymen who played cards outside the villa were listening at the entrance to what was going on in the salon. It soon became high time to break up the conversation as I had to take my horse back to Fournes. The first lieutenant gave me another cup of coffee to lessen the potent effect of the red wine and when I climbed on to my nag, I was seeing everything double but she knew the way exactly and brought me safely back to my quarters.

With the advancing of the warmer season and the dry March winds, the marshy ground at Fromelles was drying out more and more. At the beginning of April we had to reckon with an imminent enemy attack. The trenches were strengthened with a wall of sandbags. Every evening columns with reinforcement material drove to the front, where it was transferred to the trenches in rolling stock. We built bombproof dugouts and chiefly undertook everything for the safety of the garrison. For this reason, Fournes station was mainly shelled towards evening when the wagons were loaded with material. The civilians worried about the bombardment less the first time, but, in the middle of April, when a direct hit killed a family, they became more fearful, left their houses and were brought back again by arrangement of supreme command.

The column leader was glad every time when they brought their loaded wagons from the station, but also from the streets to the front line they were taken heavily under fire and it often happened that the drivers threw

One of the best-known images of Adolf Hitler taken during his time on the Western Front, this picture shows the future German leader with some of his comrades near their billets in the French village of Fournes-en-Weppes, circa August 1916. Hitler can be seen on the right of the middle row. (*Bundesarchiv, Bild 146-1974-082-44*)

One of the many paintings and drawings that Hitler completed during his service on the Western Front in the First World War. Dated December 1914, this scene is of the ruins of a Monastery in Messines.

(All images Public Domain unless stated otherwise)

Also taken in Fournes-en-Weppes, in this group photograph of members of the 16th Bavarian Reserve Infantry Regiment, at least one whom appears to be injured, Hitler can be seen on the left of the front row.

A photograph of Adolf Hitler taken during his service in the 16th Bavarian Reserve Infantry Regiment in the First World War. The original caption simply states, "In the Field".

Adolf Hitler photographed during his time at Fournes-en-Weppes.

Hitler, second from right, pictured with some of his comrades in Fromelles.

A postcard that Adolf Hitler sent from Munich to his regimental comrade Karl Lanzhammer on 19 December 1916. At that time, Lanzhammer was a cyclist with the regimental staff of the 16th Bavarian Reserve Infantry Regiment. For his part, Hitler he had just been released from hospital (having been recuperating from wounds) and was stationed with the Regiment's reserves in Munich. Hitler informed Lanzhammer of this fact, and then went on to add, "Currently I am under dental treatment. By the way I will report voluntarily for the field immediately." (*Courtesy of Europeana14-18*)

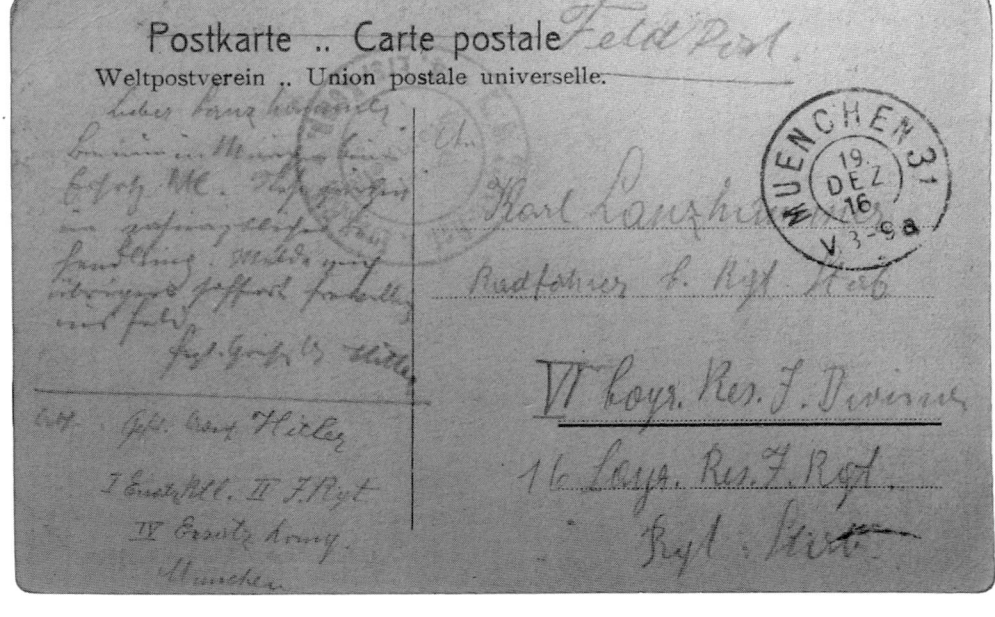

This drawing by Hitler, completed in 1917, shows the church and other buildings in the village of Ardoye (Ardooie) in the Belgian province of West Flanders.

Also painted circa 1917, this building that Hitler painted was located in the village of Fournes-en-Weppes.

Following the invasion of France in 1940, Hitler toured sections of the First World War battlefields in France and Belgium. On 1 June 1940, for example, Hitler flew to Brussels-Evere, from where he set out on a two-day tour of Belgium and Northern France. On 1 June his route was Brussels, Gent, Ypres, Langemarck and Menen. On 2 June, his route was through northern France, including stops at Vimy Ridge, where this picture was taken at the Canadian National Memorial, Arras and Cambrai. (*Historic Military Press*)

Hitler pictured leaving Langemark German War Cemetery during his tour on 1 and 2 June 1940. (*Critical Past*)

Following the invasion of France in 1940, Hitler toured sections of the First World War battlefields in France and Belgium. This picture, taken from Eva Braun's own albums, shows Hitler, accompanied by Max Amann and Ernst Schmidt, at his former billets or regimental quarters in Fournes-en-Weppes on 26 June 1940. (*NARA*)

Again from one of Eva Braun's photograph albums and taken in 1940, this picture shows a plaque that denoted one of the buildings in Fournes-en-Weppes linked to Hitler's First World War service. (*NARA*)

Hitler examines a bunker near Fromelles on 26 June 1940. The structure was one in which, the original caption notes, "he served in WW1". (*NARA*)

Also taken on 26 June 1940, this image, from one of Eva Braun's albums, is captioned as showing Hitler leaving a surviving First World War German bunker. (*NARA*)

the material into the street trenches before they reached their destination and returned with their team. Steps had to be taken, of course, to prevent this nonsense and I got the order to take to the commander of the vehicles. The drivers thought at first that I only wanted to join them and concerned themselves with me. The column leader rode behind the column and formed the rear. Near Lavarie we came under fire which wounded a horse in our team. Immediately the front driver stopped and wanted to, again, throw the material into the trenches and turn back, but this time they had miscalculated. With pistol in hand, I jumped into action and, with sharp words, I made them aware that any of them who refused to drive would be shot in front of the troop. Some of these cowards wanted to go off at me and they knew I knew no pardon and limited themselves to cursing and complaining. One said, 'You rascal, you can give up the ghost and I don't care about that, but I have a wife and children at home and I won't let myself be shot by this lie.' And with all my energy I compelled the mutineer to travel on.

Near our destination, we came under fire again, but they did not have the guts to put up any resistance. It was the same ones who did not want to go through the firing range. They boasted about it more when they were out of the danger zone. Reporting to Colonel List, I said nothing about the resistance of the two drivers. I tried only to send along a few more messengers to the next command. He knew only too well why I had made this request to him. On a different evening I accompanied the vehicle column of the 6th heavy cavalry; with that, any resistance was broken.

In the first days of May I sat together with the regimental orderlies in their recreation room. The regiment was at rest and even the messengers had less to do. Adolf Hitler talked about his favourite topics, art and painting; I listened to him gladly and was amazed how he knew about this subject. For me, this conversation was always very exciting, I could deepen my knowledge and it was refreshing to hear something once again from his civilian life. He could explain, like a professor, about German history of art. Later, we spoke about our combat sector; on this he knew the area of every strategic point of our section of the front and, later, what Adolf Hitler predicted came true. In his astuteness, he grabbed every situation and when I went forward with other messengers it often meant that if Hitler was with us, nothing happened. They counted on his intelligence and circumspection. Even his personal courage was acknowledged by those around him. He had enemies only when it came to speaking about his favourite theme, politics. In 1915 there were already comrades in his closest circle who did not share his opinion of the state and national socialism. I willingly listened to him, although, at that time, like today, politics interested me little.

Also, on this afternoon, Hitler had an intense debate with a comrade which was almost brought to a sudden ending by the explosion of an English shell. Fragments of wall flew into our quarters so we immediately ran out onto the street where our suspicion was confirmed that the shell had exploded close to the church. Now I was afraid for my horse who had her stable in the immediate vicinity. It had exploded in the garden next to the stable.

My girl stood unscathed, but pieces of the roof had fallen off and she had torn off the stable halter. At my appearance she calmed down straight away and looked at me for protection. While I cleaned away the dust and mortar, the servant girl of my host, who was pregnant, came and asked me if I could call a German doctor. Her mistress was in the cellar in the process of delivering the baby. I fetched Dr Rühl across and after a short time a little new arrival was brought up the stairs. Dr Rühl stayed close by the lady and attended to her every need. The same evening, she was taken to a civilian hospital in Houbourdin. The house where I was quartered was only slightly damaged by the explosion of the shell, but I no longer trusted the English artillerymen and looked for different accommodation. Most of the barns were filled with the 6th Bavarian field artillery regiment. I myself could have slept in the cellar which had now become free, but my second me – my horse, I could not take her down there with me. The next day the roof of my quarters was taken off, but luckily I was outside Fournes; now it was high time to disappear. I informed Sergeant Umann that I was on the look-out for different quarters for my horse. He advised me also to search for a safe place because it would be dangerous for my animal if something should happen to it. Adolf Hitler stood nearby and listened to our conversation which, once again, provided him with material to take the mickey out of me. Umann made a grim face and reprimanded Hitler, 'Don't laugh, we might perhaps have to set out from here soon if the English allow us enough time.' It was to be understood that Sergeant Umann was somewhat different in his study. Daily, the shells roared away over him and exploded close by. Several times he said to me, 'But when I report to the trenches, I am safer there than here. You need quite strong nerves and an unusually strong sense of duty with it to sit at a desk forever fulfilling your repeated duty and waiting for death or a miracle.'

That same day I had found nice quarters outside Fournes, on the road to Beaucamp, in a small mill. The owner was serving in the French army leaving his wife and only child behind. Upon my request to leave my horse in their care in the empty stable, she started crying and asked me to live with her; she was so frightened since there was no longer a man in the house. She gave me a spacious room and we not only had good accommodation but good food.

On 2 May 1915, I stood with Adolf Hitler in the courtyard of the regimental staff in Fromelles and was waiting for an order for Wavrin. The enemy shells exploded incessantly above us. The sentry in the marketplace was skiving off looking for protection behind the cross standing there; perhaps he also believed in a miracle that nothing would happen to him here. It was also a strange picture, complete houses around the crucifix had been blown out of the earth and only the figure of our saviour remained unscathed.

Hitler was just cleaning his tunic off in the courtyard when a heavy shell exploded behind the house. We were, momentarily, numb with terror. Wimmer stood next to me as pale as a corpse and out of the cellars, which the staff used as accommodation, Colonel Betz and his adjutant came running to ask where it had exploded. We were incapable of answering the colonel; only Hitler, who now was charging around his dirty courtyard, turned around with great composure as if he had started this battle. The orderlies and messengers skived off in Colonel Betz's shelter. I would have liked to look for protection but had to stay with my horse at the entrance to the cellar. Everyone felt the force of the blast; only Hitler was not among them. Someone asked, 'Where is Adolf then?' 'He's off in Fromelles looking for better boots; perhaps he has found a bucket of synthetic honey [Hitler was known to have a penchant for sugar] then he would be sat down there for a time.' General laughter.

Another thought, if you put a stable bucket full of tea with it, then you wouldn't need to bring any more until tomorrow. But it is possible to get courage from synthetic honey and tea despite the bombardment Hitler was looking for good footwear while we were hiding away in the earth. There I had seized on a sore point, and they stopped mucking about. Blow after blow followed and we waited every minute for a direct hit on our shelter. Colonel Betz didn't let me wait any longer, he sent me back to Fournes; that evening I was to report back to him. On the return ride I encountered Hitler. He had, in fact, a pair of shoes in his hand and was as calm as if he had bought them from a fair. Our Regimental Sergeant Umann, in the meantime, worked in his room where ink pots and other objects danced about.

9 May 1915

On Saturday, 8 May, Lieutenant Weissgerber sent his batman to me; I should accompany him to Chateau Ligny. Once again, he wanted to practise his horsemanship. Towards 2 in the afternoon, we rode via Beaucamp, Chateau Ligny, Chateau La Vallée to Wavrin where Lieutenant Weissgerber gave a letter to the sentry. Who would have believed this day that in 24 hours' time the famous artist and brave officer should be counted among the dead. On the way he told me that he was an artist but only occasionally in the messenger's quarters was his name called. He described Adolf Hitler to me as one of the most well-known Munich artists. He was always very friendly towards me and for this reason I also took the greatest trouble to furnish him with a horse. His slender figure and his soft hands alleviated my concerns and after a few hours of instruction, Lieutenant Weissgerber was riding as if he had been sat in the saddle for years. Before we separated on this Saturday, he gave me another handful of cigarettes. To my question about when we would go riding again, he replied, 'Dear Mend, I can't tell you that in advance, I lead a company and live from day to day.'

The 8 May passed quite peacefully, only a few salvos were heard in the afternoon at Fromelles. Towards the evening I still had to take a message up to the front. Everything was calm, only a few rifle bullets whistled past me. Despite having a good bed in my new quarters, I could not get off to sleep on the night of 8/9 May. The constant danger wears down the strongest nerves and sometimes had the effect of waking me up in bed.

At 6 o'clock in the morning when the girl had been taken care of, the front lay in deep calm. Towards 7 then, when everyone else was still asleep, I enquired at the regimental staff about my duty. Adolf Hitler, as well as the remaining messengers, lay on their canvas sheets; on the way back several civilians approached me on their way to Mass. When I passed the last house on the street to Beaucamp, I heard quite dull firing. It howled away over me as if a railway carriage was tearing through the air and fell onto the schoolhouse which, seconds before, I had passed. One could see nothing more, only the terrible cries and calls for help could be heard from the houses that remained standing and were still inhabited by civilians. When the sulphur cloud had passed, I saw civilians clothed only in a shirt and women with children in their arms running around in the street. The schoolhouse was torn out of the ground and the remains lay scattered round about. The destroyed corpses of those comrades quartered in the schoolhouse were a dreadful sight.

With this first direct hit, the terrible battle of 9 May opened. At the same time, at 7 o'clock, there was a powerful explosion to be heard around the combat zone which could have only been caused by blowing up a mine. An angry artillery duel began. The remaining German batteries at Fournes were firing everything that came out of the barrel. While I stood at the schoolhouse, a heavy shell exploded on the regimental staff building. I thought everyone would be lost as, a few minutes before, they were lying in a deep sleep. I ran back immediately to my quarters and climbed a tree to look through a telescope at our section of trench. But every attempt at orientation was impossible. The whole country was shrouded in smoke, only the burst of the shells and the flashing of shrapnel could be distinguished. Now I did not waste time, I made myself ready to ride to the staff. When my old lady saw me marching to get on to my horse, however, she started to wail and bid me to come into the cellar with her otherwise I would be shot. This assumption made me laugh and I answered her that, today, my place was elsewhere.

Having arrived at staff headquarters, Colonel Betz stood together with the commander General Kiefhaber. They were still studying the map, Colonel Betz glanced at me and said, 'It's great that you are here Mend; wait a moment you are coming with us to the front.' At the heavily damaged staff building, Adolf Hitler stood with the remaining messengers and orderlies ready to march off. As I still did not know what was happening to our regiment, I asked the messengers, and heard that the English had burst through and had penetrated our front line. Already messages were reaching the colonel about fallen comrades. Even Lieutenant Weissgerber was among the dead. Yesterday still so fresh and jolly on the ride together, today dead! The messengers and the comrades standing at the Place du Pavilion marched off to the front at intervals in pairs to avoid heavy losses.

In Fournes and our immediate surroundings, shell after shell exploded and the time until the men were ready to depart became damnably long. From the saddle of a horse, the courtyard of the regimental building could be clearly seen. Windowpanes and bricks covered the floor. I was amazed that no one from the staff had been killed; just before our column left a round ripped open the street. My horse reared up and I was injured in the eye from clods of earth hurtling through the air. I accompanied Colonel Betz and the general to just outside Lavarie. That was a journey from hell. In front of and behind us shells constantly exploded. Suddenly the column stopped, Colonel Betz waved me across and gave me a form that I had to take to the adjutant in Fromelles who had already ridden ahead. Avoiding, in a zigzag, all the shot-up main points, I reached, with my sweat-drenched horse, the staff dugout in Fromelles. The shells hailed down from Lavarie to Fromelles so that I did not believe that the column could get through. Many messengers stood in the dugout, Adolf Hitler had already gone with a message to the trench. Today he had the opportunity to prove, once again, what he was made of. That he had already been sent, as the first person, to the combat zone, proved that he was one of our best messengers. The raging drumfire strengthened once again towards midday. The English artillery laid its fire further back in order to stop reserves marching up. Already, bunches of wounded men came to the dressing station. With contempt for death, our orderlies fetched wounded comrades out of the combat zone. With the arrival of the column, our commanders went on foot into the trenches. Our adjutant sent me, again, with a message to Waverin to the waiting reserves. I saw a troop of cavalry galloping at top speed from there. They were my comrades, the other messengers. At every shell which exploded near us, the horses reared up and scattered. On their signal, I showed them the way with my sword. I turned left in the direction of Beaucamp. At an active battery I stopped. The barrels were already glowing and were wrapped with wet sacking. A non-commissioned officer, who, with a few men, was dragging shell baskets, told me that they put down their fire at the threat of an attack by a brigade of English cavalry that was standing ready. Regarding my question about how things were in Fromelles, he thought of the English who had, today, penetrated our trenches. A few more will be alive; no others will follow. The glowing oven made sure of that. 'We have already fired 800 rounds.' With a certain relief I rode on at a quick gallop. At the edge of Waverin, many troops stood ready to march to Fromelles. I asked a company commander about the major to whom I had to give the message. The officers asked their men before they went to the front in a few pithy words to do their duty. Never will I forget the calm and discipline of these reserve troops.

Having handed over my message, I turned back to Fromelles. Just outside Fournes a whole column of ambulances approached me. In the place itself, although it had been heavily shot up, munitions columns stood along the street.

As I was now without a message, I rode on at a calm pace. In Lavarie I wanted to water my horse at the battery firing there, with whose commander I had spent a pleasant afternoon. Today it looked very different from on that occasion. The first lieutenant stood, still dressed in braided trousers, behind the guns and conducted the firing. In the morning he had not had enough time to get into battle dress. With such energy he led the command; the artillery men at their guns, drenched in sweat, followed the orders of their commander to the letter. Behind the guns already lay mountains of cartridges; it was a joy to see all this working together. The men had no time to pay attention to me. Salvo after salvo was fired so that my ears rang, and I no longer dared to close my mouth.

Luckily, I reached Fromelles in one piece. I could not otherwise take care of my horse as today this stable was being used by orderlies. On the floor lay wounded white and coloured English troops. When I threw open the doors of the stable, the wounded cried out to me, 'Water please!' A coloured soldier who groaned the worst was hit in the face by his neighbour, a white Englishman; he could no longer put up with the constant cries of pain. I dragged the badly wounded Indian into the other corner of the stable and brought him water. Meanwhile, Dr Dir came with his orderlies who immediately got to work.

Adolf Hitler arrived at staff headquarters. Already many times today he had trodden the path between Fromelles and the combat zone in the heavy barrage. In a few words he gave his report: 10th company is still surrounded but Lieutenant Bachschneider was with them. The English, who this morning had penetrated our trenches, were in bitter hand-to-hand fighting with our men, however, engineers should become available in the afternoon. Every shell crater was bitterly fought over. English reinforcement was cut off due to our blocking fire. Many hung on the electric wire and cried horribly. With rifle in hand, grenades on his belt, Hitler left us. I stood with the regimental clerk who, a few days later, died on the same spot. As we both knew Hitler as a person who never exaggerated, and acquitted himself very carefully in such situations, we assumed that a bloody struggle was taking place. His awful appearance stood out to us both, he must have seen such terrible things and joined in himself. The expression in the eyes of his thin, yellowy face told us enough.

The artillery battle continued again, and again, with undiminished ferocity. The Tommies doubtlessly shot at our columns in order to hold back the reserves, while the remainder laid down an annihilating blocking fire on the English trenches. Towards 2 o'clock, our first reserves had worked their way through the firing to Fromelles. At the dressing station in the courtyard of the staff quarters it looked, in the afternoon, like a slaughterhouse. Blood stuck to the wounded like tree bark to their clothes because it was a hot day. The cries of pain went right through me, I got closer to the door to see someone whose groans of death were unbearable. He lay on a stone slab from the stable covered with his tunic.

I lifted it up and saw a coloured soldier. His head was a bloody lump of flesh with the top of the skull torn off, his lower jaw must still be lying up front in the trench. His tongue lay on his breast. I couldn't stand it any longer and ran out to my horse and cursed the war and all it stood for.

Sitting on the shaft of an ambulance I saw infantrymen and other troops all marching past on the way to the combat zone. In the evening they were supposed to be put into the counterattack. With gloomy faces, sunken eyes, sweat-soaked, but calm, they marched up to the trenches. An ambulance full of wounded stopped nearby. The commander noticed restlessness between the men and gave them an order straight away. There were many there going into action for the first time. Behind, the engineer company was pushing on from Fromelles. Apart from rifles and hand grenades, they were badly equipped for close-quarter fighting. The greater part of the company, mainly upper and lower Bavarians, were quite dangerous daredevils that could fetch the Devil from hell. Despite the heaviest firing, they sang their engineers' song.

Before nightfall I was sent on a mission to Fournes. While I was saddling my horse, messenger Dammerl came to me with a bloody nose. He came from the front and reported that our engineers found themselves in a heavy battle with the English. They fought with utter disgust, man to man and using only their spars and knives as weapons. I saw messenger Schmidt and Adolf Hitler leave the dugout again and march off to the combat zone. At the fastest gallop I rode to Fournes. There were dead comrades, smashed munitions wagons and horses with torn bodies everywhere. The battery in Lavarie fired everything out of the barrel. Their commander, 'Handsome Roland', had become hotter, due to the many orders with which he conducted the firing, and just waved with his hand when I rode past. Soon afterwards the message followed, 'target 2700', and the air pressure of the fired salvo suffocated me. In Fournes, I gave the commander my pack and non-commissioned officer Steger and Sergeant Witzgall my message. In the places where the artillery fire was less, munitions columns halted, baggage wagons along with different groups of infantries stood ready. The servicemen from the field canteens as well as the drivers had serious expressions. They also had to count on losses when they brought their field kitchens to the front.

Having arrived at my quarters, the lady, dressed in black, received me and told me, crying bitterly, that during the afternoon her brother had been killed, on the spot, by an English shell. Towards 9 in the evening, I rode to Fromelles. On the road between Fournes and Beaucamp, Saxon batteries came towards me; they were driving quickly to Radinghem.

Already the enemy artillery had significantly slackened. The will of our enemy to attack seemed to reduce. In order to avoid the badly shot-up streets, I rode across country, but this time encountered heavy gunfire. The English machine guns must have shot much too high otherwise it would not have been possible for the bullets to whistle around my eyes so far behind Fromelles. Sometimes they came so thickly that I jumped from the horse and threw myself to the floor, leaving my horse to its fate. Towards 11 in the evening, it was rather quiet, however, our artillery was firing as violently as ever. The Saxon troops had obviously been installed, for I saw, in the direction of Beaucamp–Radinghem, a constant flashing of firing guns. They flanked the enemy trenches opposite our section of the front.

In Fromelles Colonel Betz and General Kiefhaber stood outside the regimental dugout. From the few words I understood I concluded that the worst was over, and the English attack was considered at an end, however, some companies were still threatened. Major Spatny reported, however, favourably about his situation. Colonel Betz had lit up a cigar, satisfied, smiling, a sign that his strategic arrangements had led to success. When General Kiefhaber separated from the colonel I reported on the spot. I had to go off with a message to 6th Bavarian reserve field artillery regiment. I handed this over in the ruins of a farm to artillery Major Parsival, who I had knew mostly because of his skilled fire coordination which had contributed to the English defeat.

I had not seen Hitler again during the night; he stayed with a battalion at the front. After midnight I arrived at my quarters where I found Madame Dubois praying in the cellar by candlelight. She made me a strong tea and was glad when I told her that the English attack was over.

The next morning, I rode at a comfortable pace to Fromelles (the artillery fire had stopped). Apart from isolated shells which exploded from time to time, everything was calm. The sentry in the marketplace stood in front of the still undamaged cross. I put my horse in a shed and looked for Dr Dir. Comrades who came from the trenches told of the same terrible events which we had heard from Hitler some days before. It must have been a dreadful battle as the land was strewn with corpses. At the dressing station they worked feverishly. The wounded Englishmen lay in rows in the yard and in the stable. The majority demanded drinks and one of our orderlies continuously provided water and cold tea. Many who could no longer drink moistened their mouths with water. Some lay in the throes of death, others, who had been freed from their pain by injections, provided, through grateful looks, the proof that they had got to know us and we were not barbarians, as they had been led to believe by their superiors over there. Again, and again, I heard, 'Thank you, comrade.' I turned over a beanpole Highlander who had been shot in the chest and laid flat on the ground, so that he could breathe more easily. Immediately he grabbed his left hand and wanted to give me his gold ring. I always had a bit more pity for blue-eyed Englishmen than with the remainder of our enemy who disowned their race. I could also not understand how blood relations could murder each other so terribly. Perhaps I had already taken on some of the attitude of Hitler who, although he had no consideration in battle for wounded prisoners and the remaining civilians in the combat area, was always extremely considerate and kind. Towards French women he was unapproachable and would never admit to flirting, we always called him 'misogynist'. Sometimes he looked at me questioningly if I conversed with French women and I had to ignore many remarks from him. Towards midday I left Fromelles with Dr Dir. The wounded were brought back. In the combat zone the clearing up went on. From comrades I heard that, during the heavy fighting on 9 May, Hitler carried his messages through artillery and machine-gun fire and so, with absolute dedication and risk to his life, had contributed much to the victory.

Once more the soldiers' cemetery in Fournes received many new rows of little wooden crosses, but there our dead comrades could not lie in peace because the English artillery shot at it almost daily, and the buried soldiers often had to be buried again. When the regiment returned to Fournes for rest, our accommodation and quarters had been pounded into little houses. Not far from Fournes, the regiment was accommodated in barracks situated to one side of the street in the grounds of Chateau La Vallée. The orderlies moved into what had previously been a cafe, along with Hitler and myself. We stayed here over a year. During this long coexistence we had the opportunity to get to know each other even better. We got on well despite many sharp debates.

On quiet days when there was not much to do, each spent his time as they liked. Among the regimental orderlies, a great variety of jobs was represented from academic to farm labourer. The composer composed, the engineer designed and prepared himself for his later profession. The farmers told of their interests. Adolf Hitler busied himself mainly with literature and painting; with great skill he characterised Viennese Jews. Everything went peacefully until the difficult subject of politics was touched on. Then it was like a day in the Reichstag. Hitler was the orator. Most thought his political view was good and, I may say that, from 1915 to 1916, at Black Marie's in Fournes he had his first national socialist supporters around him.

There was a Jew among us, with his cosmopolitan views, who absolutely could not tolerate Hitler. For this reason, there were often differences of opinion between the two of them. I myself on one occasion had a sharp exchange of views with him.

But all in all, we got on well. Hitler filled many pleasant hours through his talent for addressing an audience and his great knowledge, but woe betide those who were inclined to mock him.

Once I attacked him with my riding boots. In the room where we slept, there were numerous rats. Hitler used to spend his time putting them to flight with his pistol if they disturbed him during the night. He lay near me and with his sudden jumping up, he hit my feet so hard that I had to cry out loudly. In my anger, I threw one of my riding boots at his head. That did not anger him, he did not let it disturb his hunting of the rats. Neither did he react to the various military pet names given him. Finally, I stopped him hunting further, we were like brothers, used to each other and accepted the other's little quirks.

Army Report, 9 May 1915

A surprising mine detonation on 9 May allowed the enemy to overrun a portion of the position of the reserve infantry regiment no. 16 and to win about 500m of ground. But here, the strength of the prepared English breach (4th English artillery regiment and parts of a territorial division) died out. While the infantrymen were engaged in bitter fighting nearby with the penetrating English soldiers, the supporting enemy formations (nearly all 4th infantry brigade) were unable to get through the highly efficient field artillery and infantry and left their forward penetrating comrades to their fate. At 7 in the evening the front line was held by reserve infantry regiment 16, whose 10th company, under the command of Lieutenant Bachschneider, had freed itself after over 12 hours of being surrounded by the enemy. The fighting, behind the line, only ended on 10 May at 5 o'clock in the morning and it was not an exaggeration to estimate enemy losses between 3,000 and 4,000 men: 2 English officers and 147 men were taken prisoner and 7 machine guns captured.

Despite the heavy defeat at Fromelles, our enemy continued his attacks on our section of the front, with greater violence and a huge commitment of troops. Chiefly at La Bassée and Richebourg, terrible firing raged. At sunset, the fighting was at its most bitter. Often you would have thought that we were in the middle of a battlefield. For days now, only the muffled rolling of the drumfire was to be heard. Smoke and clouds of sulphur darkened the horizon. All these signs showed us that it would not be long before we were alerted, and so it was. After a week, on 17 May, a section of our regiment entrained for La Bassée. During the same day, the English attacked our position once again and the German parts of the front line trenches were snatched away. At midnight from 17 to 18 May, the threatened section was asked to support the neighbouring division for which we sent, during the night, all available reserves; six companies of 6th Bavarian reserve division. Their timely arrival and their bravery in the face of the initially superior English attack succeeded in stopping the threatened breakthrough until stronger forces were brought up.

While in Galizien, our united armies rushed from victory to victory; the army of the Crown Prince of Bavaria, which also belonged to our division, had a battle to win that was no less fierce and bloody. There were no assault troops here because of the rows of enemy, no pursuit of retreating divisions but our troops had the difficult task of putting a stop to our enemy attackers. At that time our enemy didn't just want to divert the strength of our spent armies in Galizien, but also force a breakthrough to the German lines in the West. General Joffre considered that, at that time, the moment had arrived to break through the German front, which would liberate the occupied provinces and Belgium, and carry the war into the Rhineland. The scene of the breakthrough was the area around La Bassée. The strategic situation appeared favourable for the plan. The positions of our troops were not carefully selected for defence, but just the positions that they had occupied for the offensive. In the almost flat area of Flanders, between the district of Armentières and La Bassée, there was a pronounced advantage in terrain in the Tommies' hands. However, there were, at La Bassée, many prominent parts of our line from which an encircling of the enemy was quite possible. Also, every attack of our enemy was favoured because of the lack of vision through the thickly planted trees. At the big battle of 17 and 18 May, I was sent, on the second day, with a message from Fournes to La Bassée. However, I had to hurry straight back. On my ride over there I met many civilians who had to leave behind all of their possessions. Wounded people told me of the terrible fighting and English attacks; most no longer believed that we could hold back the onslaught of the Allies any longer.

During these days I did not see Adolf Hitler but, later, he told me of the terrible fighting. The breakthrough was stopped by the immediate help of our regiment as much as other formations; but the losses were even worse than on 9 May.

On the way from Violain to La Bassée (although up to 10km behind the combat zone) shells positively rained down. In a small farm, not far from Billy, civilians were busying themselves cutting off the rear parts of some shot-up horses still joined as a team. An old French lady clicked her tongue and thought 'that's a good beef steak'. The dressing station in Fromelles resembled a slaughterhouse. Inside and outside all the cemeteries, the dead lay piled up on top of each other. Not far from Bouvin, on the cemetery wall, there were thirty-seven dead alone. I let my horse have a breather and watched the orderlies busy digging graves. In the wide-open mass grave there lay, on the bottom row, thirty dead. They were sprayed with chalk, a film of straw laid on them and prepared for another layer. My question to the orderlies busying themselves there concerning how many dead would be buried in this mass grave was answered with, up until this evening we have brought another 100 together. I rode back outside the firing to Fournes and was glad to reach my quarters and to be able to calm my nerves.

The decimated companies turned back to Fournes and took up their old positions at Fromelles where they were in a state of high readiness for another English attack. Our regiment suffered at times from increased artillery fire which our enemy covered from our front line to Wavrin (15km) resulting in daily losses.

Towards the end of July 1915, in the afternoons I sat with Adolf Hitler and the other messengers in our quarters. It was quiet at the front but even more lively with us. That afternoon, we had our fun with a messenger, a hop farmer. The latter admired Hitler a lot and what he said was gospel to him. At this time our hop farmer had taken a letter from the home of a resident baron there to which he had to respond. That presented obstacles for him, so he asked Hitler whether he would like to draft a letter which would be fitting for such a high-standing figure. With many jokes and humour Hitler dictated the letter so that we all had to laugh especially when, throughout, he made his funny comments to us. Later, I went into the canteen at the church but only stayed a little while; that was lucky because, that evening, another shell exploded there. A minute before the explosion Hitler went past with a message and he, and I, escaped death once again. It was all just destiny and a matter of chance.

For example, a sapper was fishing in the moat of the Chateau du compte d'Hespel. While he calmly held his rod in the water he was torn apart by a shell. Even the earlier mentioned First Lieutenant 'Handsome Roland' who directed his battery during various battles under heavy fire, and remained unscathed, was torn to pieces by a flying bomb while bathing at Wavrin.

One evening I was riding with a message from Fournes to Beaucamp. The artilleryman stationed in the monastery had butchered a pig and invited me to try their boiled pork belly. While I sat eating, a sergeant arrived and asked whether the horse that was rolling around in the open fields behind the monastery belonged to me. He had tried to catch her but had not been successful. The horse was covered in dirt and the saddlebags were lying in the clover. I said, 'Yes, that's my horse; if she discovers a field of clover, she likes to have unauthorised trips.' I left my food and looked for my horse who, when she saw me coming, rolled around high spiritedly on the ground. After a while, I ran after her. Suddenly I heard firing and a shell howled above my head. It exploded in front of the stable in which my horse, along with two other artillery horses, had stood. Both horses were dead, and a rider had been badly wounded by a splinter. The battlefield feast had been forcefully ended. In the canteen cauldron was a potpourri of bricks, mortar and earth, fat and bits of meat. The artillerymen moaned and swore and conspired that, at the catching of next pig, they would carefully make up the feast.

On 14 July, the French national holiday, Adolf Hitler met me at the town hall. He was on the way to Fromelles with a message. We only exchanged a few words and then separated. The next moment a heavy shell struck the town hall. A lady who had not wanted to leave her house was killed by shell splinters. Hitler told me in the evening that bits of iron flew away over his head and he was glad to leave Fournes.

On the same day things were hot in Fromelles as, since early morning, the place lay under artillery fire. The Allies wanted to give the French national day a special aura by the destruction of many Bosches. A few days later, when I left in the morning with a message for Fromelles, Hitler stood around with his comrades and we joked together. Most of them were busying themselves, in their free time, getting wood to make tea and coffee. They had, nevertheless, often abandoned the fire with the shelling of Fournes, but none of them had suffered any damage. I set off on my way and, on the way back, at Rosewood Farm, an engineer approached me and told me that an orderly had been killed at regimental staff. Who was the unlucky soul then? The regimental clerk had caught it when he had left his dugout, standing for a few minutes in the open air stopping the messengers.

One Sunday I went with Hitler through the streets of Fournes to church. Hitler had, in his pocket, a report for the brigade staff in Chateau du compte d'Hespel. At the church we separated, I went to Colonel Betz; he was still speaking with a comrade. Colonel Betz was just in the process of giving me an order when a heavy shell went over us and exploded quite close, so that the, until now, preserved windowpanes in his quarters fell into a thousand fragments on the plaster.

In front of the commander I tried to hide my terror as well as I could but even his hand trembled while writing. From the window we saw soldiers sprinting towards the church where the shell had exploded. I commented to Colonel Betz that, a few minutes ago, Adolf Hitler had been standing with an infantryman at the church. The colonel interrupted me, grabbed me by the arm and shoved me to the door with the words, 'Just look what has happened'. I came out and saw the church steps covered with blood. In the corners lay bits of the bodies of two artillerymen. There was nothing to be seen of Hitler and his comrade. Seconds before, they must have left the spot. The soldiers who had congregated in front of the church had seen the two of them speaking and were amazed that they had got away earlier.

I reported to Colonel Betz and rode to Houbordin. In the evening outside the regimental office, I said to Hitler, 'My dear chap, just one minute longer today at the church square and, instead of two, we would have had four dead.' Adolf Hitler shook his helmet from his head and said, 'We would have' and disappeared through the doors.

One room on the upper floor of Major Spatny's quarters was inhabited by a young lady lawyer with three delightful girls, from whose window she often watched the goings on of the street. One day, as she later told me, she had an inkling in the morning that she should transfer to the cellar with her children. It did not really cause any worry because the firing was no heavier than usual, but an inexplicable compulsion caused her to act like this. And in fact, on the same day, a 38.5-tonner scored a dreadful hit on the street in front of the house. Her room was completely demolished.

A few days later, the young woman was again favoured by luck, as the same battery of English navy guns sent their shells to Fournes. One of them hit her house. Immediately a junior officer, who I knew well, hurried into the cellar to rescue her and her children from the rubble. He was able to remove the children but during an attempt to rescue the mother, he met his fate. A second shell killed him on the spot. The infantrymen who had noticed the incident managed to enter the cellar and got the mother out with great threat to life. Because of this brave act, the three children and their mother were rescued but a young German soldier had given up his life for it.

The grand nation, which could lay claim to chivalry, knows to report nothing of these and many thousands of similar situations but if Germans like Remarque and Förster sully their own nest, what can you expect from the hereditary enemy?

Even in this shelling, Hitler escaped with his life. Many a comrade will say, perhaps, 'Hitler has had it much better than us as a regimental orderly.' He had good quarters and never had to stay in the trenches, while we, with our soaked clothes, had to wait on the front line. I agreed with the orderlies who were always at the front and said to me that they would rather have stayed in the trenches than now having to jump through the fire without cover.

July passed calmly, by a fluke. There were always wounded and dead, mainly when relieved companies lamented their losses. Towards the end of the month Fromelles was again heavily shelled and I often noticed that messengers did not agree whose turn it was if someone called from the regimental office. Mainly then, if the house trembled again through heavy shelling, it would be better if no one got up. So it was that Hitler, without being asked, moved away secretly, and brought the message.

As the others had agreed, Adolf Hitler was already underway with the order about which few were pleased. Again, I made the other messengers understand that it was uncomradely for one person to always run with the message. They answered me, 'If Hitler is so stupid, we are not.'

As soon as it got hot at the front, Hitler behaved like a racehorse before the start. He then had the habit of wandering around restlessly, buckling up to get himself ready. That often got on the others' nerves, especially if they were sitting cosily in their quarters and were glad not to be called.

One day I went for a walk with Hitler on the street. The way to Lavarie, which we had to take, had just been shot up. I was curious how Hitler behaved and wanted to see with my own eyes whether he was really the courageous one, for which, in general, he had been taken for. This way there were radio operators busy laying out telephone wires. Then, quite close to Hitler, a salvo exploded. I preferred to talk to the telephonists and wait for the firing to stop but Hitler continued on his merry way as cool as a cucumber. But now I did not want to blame myself, for, if Hitler had seen, I would not have escaped his ridicule and so I bade him farewell with the comment that, up ahead, our best messenger was walking, which certainly made me feel cowardly as I did not follow him. One of the telephonists knew Hitler from earlier and thought, 'The nutcase will tie his shoelace, wait for the firing to stop and walk through hell.' I did not do that but went at a fast pace until I had caught up with him. We often had to go through such hail of iron so that all curiosity about Hitler's behaviour on patrol faded.

By August 1915 you heard no more jokes being cracked by the regimental orderlies in Hitler's presence, and when the situation was so precarious. On another occasion, I happened to witness his cold-bloodedness. The street from Fournes to Ullies lay, for the most part, under heavy artillery fire but, on this day, calm reigned and I wanted to take advantage of this to get a supply of oats directly from the field for my horse. My horse was happily close by. I saw Adolf Hitler from afar, recognisable by his swift pace. Suddenly I heard firing and saw Hitler no more. But this time, or so I thought, it had torn him to pieces. My blood went cold, but I did not trust my eyes. Who should be running again to the entrance of the village but Adolf Hitler and I was glad, this time, to know he had again come through unharmed. In the evening in our quarters, I said to him, 'Wow, the Tommies have to hammer a nail into your head if they want to kill you. With your nut there is nothing you can't achieve'. He asked me, amazed, 'Why, what happened?' as if he was not the slightest bit interested. The incident of this afternoon just was not important to him.

I was on the way from Waverin to Fournes. Suddenly, an English plane was shot down in flames by one of our anti-aircraft batteries. When the aircraft crashed from 2,000ft to the ground, the craft was completely burnt out and the two English pilots presented a horrible sight which I will never forget. Arriving in Fournes, most of the messengers hurried to the spot where the pilots had crashed, only Adolf Hitler was uninterested, and remained so following my report about what had happened. I could not understand his strange behaviour, he was, and remained, an exceptional case.

During August, we were subjected to considerable harassing fire. Tommy wanted to feign deliberate attacks through such armed assaults. Essentially the English were just intent on stopping our entrenchment work and the bringing up of material. The 6th Bavarian division's section of the front was securely entrenched because material was unloaded in Fournes by the wagonload, put into sacks and brought to the front, where it was filled with sand and the parapet strengthened. For this reason, our division in 1915 was called 'The Sandbag Division'. The population in Fournes was greatly intrigued about where all this very good material came from and complained about the German waste, although they largely got their fair share from our people. Many a lady had a cupboard full of clothes which had been made from sandbag material.

Adolf Hitler said to me occasionally that in a shot-up house in Fromelles, near the brewery, there were many balls of wool. One day, I made my way over there to fetch wool. Madame Dubois knew how to knit good stockings and I wanted to take advantage of this opportunity. Soon, without being seen, I had reached the house where hundreds of balls of wool lay everywhere. Quickly I filled my sack full and tried to go back the same way that I had come but, on the edge of Fromelles, engineers were sitting playing cards and I did not want to pass them with my sack.

I considered for a long time what I should do. Determinedly, I hid my wool sack and went towards them, waiting for the end of their game. One of them still had three rounds, although at any minute a direct hit was to be expected. They gave me cigarettes and invited me to join the game. The shelling became even more violent, one shell after another howled away over us but my engineers made no effort to end the game. One engineer attended to his wounds with his handkerchief but soon afterwards we really had to stop. A heavy English calibre shell flew over us and exploded in the nearby house. The air pressure threw us to the floor and dirt and bricks rained down on us. I came away with a slight eye injury while an engineer had a big hole in his head.

A few stalwarts collected the cards together and wanted to carry on, but it was not possible. One of them, very angrily, threw the cards onto the floor, not understanding that one could not play on because of a wounded 'kohlrabi' ['German Turnip'], as he called him. Now, finally, I could fetch my sack and go back to Fournes. My wounded eye was painful, and a few juicy explosions nearby made me run. It was most definitely too many risks for a sack of wool.

Madame Dubois was as pleased as a child when she saw so much wool, and I gave her the majority. For that she knitted me a half-dozen stockings. Hitler and the remaining messengers never learnt how I came about my wounded my eye or that I had visited the wool mill in Fournes.

At the end of August 1915, the English artillery strengthened their fire on our section of the front, and also our barrage balloon was partly bombarded by long-distance fire. Today, I had two messages to take:

one for the regimental staff in Fromelles, the other to Chateau Ligny. Behind a willow bush at the side of the road, a troop of officers from our division met me. With their binoculars they were looking for the enemy ground and, from their behaviour, it was obvious that they could observe something interesting about the enemy. From my horse, it was also possible for me, with the naked eye, to recognise enemy transport vehicles. I heard our division commander General Scanzoni, in preparation, say to an adjutant, 'We need to make our artillery aware of that.'

The General Staff then rode on at a gallop in the direction of Radinghem–Beaucamp. I hurried with my message to get away from our artillery attack. In Fromelles I met Adolf Hitler who told me about a pair of dashing English observers. When he had arrived with his message in the trenches in the morning, our artillery had bombarded an English observation post.

The latter was discovered in a tree on the side of a mountain. Although shell after shell exploded above their heads, they did not retreat but calmly observed with their telescope until one after the other was sent tumbling from the tree. Before I rode away from Fromelles, Adolf Hitler was sent, once again, to the trenches, 'Be careful an attack is coming soon', I warned him. But without replying he left with a determined look on his face. There must have been something important for him at the front. It was a question of habit for him to reach the trenches with difficult obstacles. If he did not have to go through fire, he often said on his return, 'Today, I would have been able to run in front of an old lady.' With my second message I came past a battery at Radinghem where an artilleryman said that in an hour an attack would be made on the assembly point of the English front. Many troops had been observed there by our pilots.

At a gallop I went on to Chateau Ligny. Above me an English plane, which had been heavily bombarded by our anti-aircraft batteries, circled. It glided calmly over Chateau Ligny as if the bombardment had not disturbed it; probably his observer wanted to examine the castle, in which many of our staff were, closely. Suddenly I saw flames in the air. The plane had received a direct hit and was set ablaze. One of the occupants jumped immediately out of the burning aircraft and plunged 1,500m from the plane falling into the castle grounds at Ligny. His body was partly hung from one of the poplar trees standing in the park, the other pilot burned with the plane and lay charred with his machine on the ground.

The English must already have noticed the drama because straight away heavy artillery fire attacked Beaucamp. I didn't linger long with the burned pilot because I had to get, via Beaucamp, back to my quarters at Fournes.

At the monastery at Beaucamp, the drivers wanted to hitch their horses to the munitions wagon when a heavy shell struck the monastery killing a driver and seriously wounding three horses. A large splinter struck a wall near me and tore a large hole in it even though I was more than 100m away from the point of impact. The bombardment of the monastery had brought a few of the civilians who still remained there out on to the street. They stood together gesticulating. A hysterical old lady clenched her fist at me as I rode past and hollered at me. She taunted me, saying that the pilot which we had shot down was now avenged. 'Sir, that is the revenge for the poor Englishmen.' An old man standing nearby murmured, 'Just as in 1870, that is war.' He showed me his deformed hand with the comment, 'memory of the war of 1870 at Orleans'. The old man would certainly have wanted to be a soldier again. As he moved away from me, he assumed a military posture and saluted, his trembling, deformed hand resting on his cap. Never deny a soldier's blood!

Near my quarters I met a crowd of young French boys wearing German soldiers' caps and armed with wooden sabres. The biggest of them commanded, when I rode up to them, 'Attention, stand still, eyes right.' Their heels clicked together like our recruits on the parade ground. I took pleasure in the boys and to my question, they answered in good German. They begged for cigarettes, I threw one to each of them and soon they were smoking like the home guard. On my return journey, their leader commanded again, 'Attention, stand still, section march' and they sang the song *'Lippe Detmold eine wunderschöne Stadt'*. The boys marched on in Prussian goose-steps.

In Fournes I reported to Sergeant Umann at the office. He was flustered, for all day the English shelling had disturbed him in his quarters. The shell holes behind the house were evidence of it. In the messenger's quarters, only Jackal and a messenger of the second battalion were in attendance. Everyone else was at the front. Jackal had just arrived with the news that an acquaintance had fallen, and that Hitler had also nearly got it in the approach trench. With a proud gesture, Jackal told how he had to jump through the fire. On my ride to the quarters, I crossed the cemetery. There had just been the funeral of six infantrymen of 17th Bavarian reserve infantry division. General Kiefhaber had given our fallen comrades the last rites and commemorated them with touching words. I remained sitting on my horse during the solemn ceremony. At the retreat of our infantry section, a murderous artillery fire started up. Ours laid a withering counter fire on the English reserve positions and, after a short time, the English responded. It was a particularly heavy barrage. The English also shot at Fournes. It was high time for me to leave the cemetery, as nearby enemy shells were exploding. Days afterwards, I spoke with Adolf Hitler about the attack. During the bombardment he had thrown himself to the ground behind a wall in Fromelles, read a book and observed how the English shells exploded one after another behind the village in the meadows. I wanted to give some more examples that showed the spirit that breathed life into our regiment. Never have I heard such pitiful cries from female mourners as those Remarque, in his book *All Quiet on the Western Front*, used to depict German soldiers, although I, as a despatch rider, have come into contact with many units. It is regrettable that it is the Germans who take Remarque's fantastical creation seriously.

Humour came into its own in the worst circumstances. Almost every Sunday afternoon, at 2 o'clock, you could count on a bombardment. The troops paid no attention; even less when they were planning something amusing like, for example, a Bavarian folk dance. In the garden behind a house, they made merry-go-rounds out of cartwheels and with singing, dancing and music-making passed the time away. As a jolly mountain dweller played the harmonica, a shell exploded and killed three of the comrades assembled there; many others were wounded. The play area was only empty for a short time as I saw, after some time, from my quarters, they again congregated and the dancing and music-making began anew. One of them who had taken a bit of the shell even stood there with a bandaged head. He went back onto the wagon wheel carousel and didn't let his joy be diminished.

Rosewood Farm lay constantly under fire. That didn't motivate the troops, lying in their quarters there, to desert their shelter. In my free time, I often went looking for oats and once happened upon this farm. Artillerymen and radio men sat in the badly shot-up stables playing cards. We talked – most knew me – and were in the best spirits, as came to the attention of the Tommies. The howling above didn't disturb us particularly as one of the artillerymen passed round another full bottle of cognac. We lay on this grass mound behind the thick walls of the farm, and it would need a direct hit to chase us away from here. We became more and more joyful and joined in the song '*Vom schwarzen Kragen*'. During the second verse at the point it said 'for already in the seven-year war, Fritz has gained many victories with his artillerymen' a dud landed in the manure pit next to the stable and we were showered with liquid manure. This impolite interruption did not move us from the grass mound. One of the radio men, a student in civilian life, jumped onto a munitions wagon and made a drunken speech to the Tommies, who we no longer found to be dignified and fighting according to the normal ways of war but splattering us with liquid manure in order to send the German Huns to the other side with an evil aroma. He had not yet finished his speech when a second shell exploded behind the residential building in a turnip field. The air pressure made the speaker shake and fall backwards into the munition boxes. Gradually I had had enough of this and I took my knapsack and disappeared on the pretext that I had to go now as otherwise I would have nothing to feed my horse with. The others remained lying on the grass mound rolling themselves up like a hedgehog and sleeping it off.

It was September when static warfare started again but all the signs were there that soon bigger attacks from our enemy would follow, because the fire got stronger day by day. The way from Fromelles to the front became ever more dangerous. The despatch riders were not envied. Hitler often looked very much the worse for wear, his nerves gave way, but he had pulled himself together again. The meat rations became smaller and when others were indignant about it, Hitler said to them that they should not forget that the French in 1870 consumed rats. I never saw him receive a parcel, he never accepted anything although we often offered. Every time he always changed the conversation; he did not want to know anything about leave, the trenches and Fromelles were his world and whatever lay behind that didn't exist for him.

Long Hans

One afternoon I sat with Hitler and the remaining orderlies in the quarters in Fournes. Hitler talked to us, as ever, about his favourite topics of art and painting. Suddenly there followed a terrible explosion and we rushed out into the street on the assumption that Fournes was being shelled. We heard again in the street a terrible howling in the air, it had to be from one of our heaviest shells. The shell came from Lille and, as we could no longer hear the explosion, it must have exploded far behind the enemy front. We stood puzzled. Was it the shell from one of our biggest guns? We recognised the powerful air pressure but where was the gun? None of us had seen the monster, although I, as despatch rider, was familiar with the whole area. Now, a second shell followed whose effect was not nearly so long. The gun which had fired the second shell stood in the main street of Houbordin and fulfilled the aim of deceiving the enemy about the position of the artillery. At Wavrin the balloon had been put out to observe the effect of the heavy shell. Again, a shot followed from the heavy gun and after it the phantom gun fired again. The enemy must have got some of the heavy shell because straight away enemy planes came over Fournes and the balloon at Wavrin was so heavily bombarded that it had to be taken down. After a while, Adolf Hitler came with the news that the big gun, known as 'Long Hans', had just fired two shots at Béthune station which stood far behind the French front, about 35 to 40km away from us. The pilots would have noticed that the shell had exploded in the railway station in which many troops were gathered and must have been dreadfully affected.

    I had the opportunity, two years ago (1929) when I visited the German cemeteries at Arras, to also go to Béthune. The inhabitants told me about the terrible devastation caused by heavy German shelling in 1915. Straight after the first shell in Béthune, a terrible panic ensued. Many of the population fled and in the railway station there were masses of dead civilians and soldiers.

    Another day, the guns of the English artillery were trained on Wavrin. They bombarded the railway line in whose vicinity the mortars had fired. I did not rest at this news, I wanted to see this titanic gun and intended, as soon as I came back to Houbordin with a message, to make a detour to Santes which was not very far away. A few days ago, I had received from the marines I had met in Santes the information about where 'Long Hans' was to be found. I tethered my horse and then went on foot looking for the giant gun. In a shot-up factory building, there stood on the concrete floor was this monster with its many metres-long barrel. In a concrete burrow next to it lay the many hundreds of heavy shells which had been flung onto rolling stock to the gun. It was guarded by two men; the other squad on guard and the servicers of the gun were accommodated in a barracks and stood in readiness. On a lone poplar tree, the highest observation post had been constructed to which a binocular periscope for the observation of the effects of the shells had been fixed. The French population squinted with worried eyes at the spot where the massive German gun stood built into the concrete. In the cafes they told of the dangers that the population was exposed to with the firing of this gun. At the first shot, many inhabitants had lost their hearing, pregnant women delivered prematurely and in the surrounding area of the gun, houses collapsed from the powerful air pressure. The houses nearby were vacated. Myself, as a front-line soldier, was pleased about this giant and with great satisfaction climbed onto my horse for the return journey. The English must have trembled before this giant because after a few days Santes was bombed. Fortunately, the gun was spared and, in the meantime, we were able to hear 'Long Hans' in the ensuing battles at Fromelles. When, another day, I told Hitler that I had been in Santes and had viewed the heavy gun, he sat in the corner of our lounge, head between both hands, deep in thought. Suddenly he jumped up and ran anxiously round saying that despite the big guns, victory was still denied, the invisible enemies of the German nation would be more dangerous than the biggest enemy cannons. Hitler had had a powerful political argument with a comrade. If us messengers at that time had suspected the exit from the war, perhaps we would have understood Adolf Hitler's comments and political pessimism better.

The English strengthened their artillery activity against our section of the front and shelled many villages which had remained untouched by previous bombardments. If they really wanted to attempt a breakthrough at Fromelles, they would have to get a move on because of the incoming wet season and in view of the marshy ground, any anticipated success later would have remained in vain. Don station was heavily bombarded. In the evening when we heard a muffled rumbling in the air, we knew already that it was a case of an English greeting for Don. Aerial combats were interesting if a German squadron fought the enemy close by. As soon as the pilots clashed together, the artillery fire would stop and the machine guns in the planes then began with their tack-tack-tack. I was often amazed at our squadrons whose persistence pestered the enemy and who didn't get driven away by the considerably stronger enemy until one of them was brought or shot down. We were pleased if an enemy plane was forced down unwillingly! I was once present when an English pilot was compelled to land by two German airplanes. The enemy plane came down undamaged; one of the two pilots was wounded. When both the Englishmen had been taken prisoner by us, they behaved as if they were on the sports field. They passed their papers to the German captain and told him, in a humorous way, about their misfortune as if they had never been our enemy. The wounded English officer was given an emergency dressing and accompanied by two German officers they were taken to Houbordin. I was able to observe a persistent air combat between a German and English pilot at Radinghem. Unfortunately, the German was so badly injured, by a shot to the stomach, that he had to land and went down at the brickworks at Radinghem. Shortly after he had landed his plane unscathed, he died without saying a word; one hand on the steering wheel, the other clamped on his wound. At that time, I was the first one with my horse to reached the aeroplane after it landed.

After the war, I read now and again in different scandal rags of our enemy that their officers who were unlucky to be taken prisoner were treated inhumanely, and the dead were buried like animals. On the contrary, so much kindness was often shown there. Adolf Hitler recorded clearly at the burial ceremony of an English officer in Fournes that enemy officers were buried with full military honours and, as with our fallen comrades, very little in terms of escort and solemnity were spared. Twice I was with Adolf Hitler at the burial of an English pilot. In civilian life, such burials would be granted to English officers and called burials first class. All officers present in Fournes walked in service uniform behind the coffin. In front of these marched the band, playing Chopin's 'Funeral

March'. At the grave itself, they played 'Praise the Heavens, The Eternal Honour' and the padre gave a moving funeral oration.

In Fournes, during off-duty hours, we often sat together in comfort and, if Hitler was present the conversation usually quickly developed into a high political discussion. It is a good thing that because of the racial and political opposites in the old Danube monarchy that a fierce interest for politics was awakened early in his youth.

Hitler felt High German, and much persistent Marxism, were undercurrents in these intense verbal battles. For, at that time, Hitler already saw everything from a high standpoint and through the logic of his justification, which he often couched in humorous terms, even his most dogged opponents had to agree with him. Such people were even more dear to him, the half-hearted and absentminded brothers; like, for example, a telephonist who said to him, before the big autumn battle, that it was all the same to him if Germany lost or won the war. Hitler was so angry at this that, if he had not restrained himself at that time, the telephonist would have been transported to the field hospital with a bloody head.

Chateau La Vallée

This castle lay immediately behind Fournes. The whole summer this beautiful manor house with its extensive park was spared enemy bombardment, and much of our troop's equipment and columns of vehicles were accommodated there.

In the castle itself a casino had been constructed. The orderlies behaved like royal court lackies and they, and their officers, led a life like a bird on hemp seed. There were many such types, in some legation or other, who did duty behind the front and had very little understanding of the real war. I often came to the castle and saw tables covered with the most varied selection of delicacies while the trench garrison had to put up with scarce rations. This garrison then came to La Vallée to rest, and the turnout and presumptuous tone which prevailed there caused friction. I heard from many of our front-line officers that their sole wish would be if only the enemy would send a shell into this nest of feasting.

One day when I came back from the trench garrison, many of the dissatisfied soldiers ganged up and forced entry with rifles and hand grenades where the lords were just sitting around with fat cigars and aromatic coffee. The men sharply asked them their opinion about this life behind the lines, and then moved away without letting themselves get carried away with acts of violence.

Naturally, they were brought to book for this action against the officers but, as far as I remember, not much fuss was made about it. On another day, officers and men left the castle. As my quarters in Fournes had been shot to pieces during my absence – Madame Dubois happened to be with her children in one of their fields at the time – I made up a stable in a barracks in Chateau La Vallée and stayed most of the time with Adolf Hitler and the other orderlies. When I told Hitler about the incident in the castle, he was very pleased that these base wallahs had had to exchange their calm life for another, probably less pleasant.

25 September 1915

Extract from the army report:

On 25 September, the English attacked our right flank. 20th Bavarian reserve infantry regiment pushed forward to the second line. After dreadful drumfire and gas attack, the enemy fell back upon the front trenches, but we just as quickly succeeded in sealing the point of penetration. The batteries of 6th reserve division and 6th Bavarian infantry regiment, through their well-led fire, cut off the invaders from their lifeline. The reserve companies of the infantry regiments succeeded, together with the remains of the front-line garrison, in trapping the enemy in a pincer movement and again, before darkness, many had been taken prisoner. 20th Bavarian infantry regiment had significant losses to mourn, 18 officers and 500 men. Admittedly, those of the enemy were far worse, in front of and in the position 1,000 alone were counted.

On the morning of 25 September, I rode out, in foggy weather, with a message to Fromelles. Suddenly I had a violent itching sensation in my nose and soon afterwards I had difficulty breathing. As the enemy had not yet used gas against us, I couldn't immediately tell if this is what it was. But when the itching became worse and the scent of gas became noticeable, I immediately returned. In Lavarines I saw the men forcing on gas masks and servicing their guns. Now it was a case of me, as quickly as possible, fleeing the gas cloud. I had already seen the latter high over Fournes, but behind the village on the way to Chateau La Vallée there was again much of it to swallow. Having arrived at the castle I fetched my gas mask and rode immediately back to Fromelles.

I stopped at the orderlies' quarters in Fournes, which were empty. Black Marie, their French hostess, told me that the skinny, dark-haired man (Adolf Hitler) and the blonde man (Schmidt) had, immediately after the English had started to fire so violently, marched to the front. As I knew that the orderlies, apart from Hitler who had already taken his equipment with him, had no gas masks with them, I was very worried about them. Black Marie must have also smelled a little gas because she urgently requested a gas mask from me. But I could not fulfil her wish and advised her only to hold her nose. Already behind Fournes, the gas was gradually dispersing.

Just outside Fromelles dreadful artillery fire started, our guns firing angrily into the breach in the section of the front of 20th Bavarian reserve infantry regiment. The English were also moving their fire there. In the regimental dugout of our commander there was no one apart from the clerk and a telephonist. Colonel Betz had gone with his adjutant to the front because our regiment was expecting an attack. Hitler had the difficult task of establishing a connection between 16th and 20th Bavarian reserve infantry regiments because telephone communications had been destroyed by the furious fire.

When one of our telephonists said to me that Hitler was 'connections officer', I let everyone know there was hope for him because, among our adjutants who had come from the front, I had experienced that the trenches were quite levelled out and the greatest part of the garrison was dead and buried. The telephonist thought, rolling a cigarette, we didn't need to worry about Hitler. If nobody else came through, he would. During our conversation, the adjutant of our brigade commander stepped into the dugout. After looking at my message he sent me on to brigade staff. At the quickest gallop, I rode there, at any minute an armed enemy attack could happen. From the batteries at Lavarie that were firing, which due to a direct hit had already lost some of their artillery men, shell after shell was fired at the enemy. Territory which had been taken from the enemy in the morning, was now a mass grave for the English.

Although during static war the troops complained at lot, they were, as soon as the firing started again, in their element and held their position with dogged skill. An artillery captain told me once that often no artillery man was more worried about the success of a bombardment than he himself. 'When you are at rest you constantly have something to moan about but in dangerous moments I can completely rely on you.'

When I arrived at the brigade staff, engineers were bringing in about seventy prisoners, among them many Indians. An officer allowed the prisoners to stand up and having taken their papers, he gave, in English, permission for them to lay down and rest because they looked the worse for wear. Firstly, the officers then the others were interrogated using an interpreter. While I waited for my answer, I stayed in the garden by the prisoners. An infantryman brought an Indian back there who had been interrogated. The white Englishmen assumed that he had betrayed something important to the general, they made towards him and swore at him. Suddenly they fell on him, beat him and threw him to the floor so that our guards had to intervene. The Englishmen were immediately separated from the Indians and taken behind the castle, so a further confrontation would be avoided. With signs and gestures, they thanked us for our help and, with snarling teeth and clenched fists, showed their anger towards their white comrades. A German speaking Englishman, who had stood by indifferently during the fighting, said that before the attack the coloured troops had argued with his men. One of our engineers told him, in a lower Bavarian dialect, that he was pleased when the black devils beat up the last ones, but the Englishman shook his head, 'What does last one mean?'

Towards midday the English were trapped in a pincer movement on broken ground by a company of 20th Bavarian reserve infantry regiment, under the command of Lieutenant Schönborn. Despite the most fortified resistance and the greatest bravery, the enemy was not capable of denying us.

With the return message I rode, via Fournes, back to Fromelles. The weather had cleared but smoke and clouds of sulphur pervaded the countryside. Captain von Richthofen was weaving with his squadron for hours above the combat zone, through the heavy enemy fire and held the enemy pilots in check.

In the afternoon I was sent from Houbordin to Division. Not far from Beaucamp dead artillerymen lay beside their gun and the second in command directed the fire although he a bandaged head. Despite the intense pain, the heavily wounded battery leader had taken over the position. Riding on I heard once again, 'First gun, by the right, fire.' On the track across the fields from Radinghem to Beaucamp, I stumbled upon an ambulance column. As members of the same, although badly wounded, were carried on their stretchers, behind it marched a whole column of comrades with bandaged heads and arms. Many were only clad in shirt and trousers; their tunics had been left up at the front because of their wounds. Some had also had their sleeves cut off and the blood seeped through the dressings. One orderly whose strength had deserted him, so that he could no longer support his load, was relieved by an infantryman who, himself, had a serious arm wound.

Just before the brickworks, on a range of hills in a solitary house, the dressing station was constructed. Whole columns of ambulances stood outside it. Inside, next to the badly wounded lay many with gas poisoning, blue froth on their lips.

On the plateau above, the road from Radinghem led to Houbordin, and here I came under heavy artillery fire, so I encouraged my horse on at top speed. However, she injured a foot during the gallop so I had to stop off at a forester's lodge to bandage it. Along the heavily shelled ridge I saw a munitions column travelling at a fast gallop. My horse's injury was not serious so, a short time later, I had reached Division headquarters in Houbordin and delivered my message. I rode then to Fournes without stopping.

Close by Chateau Ligny, angry drumfire started anew. In the meantime, a dreadful explosion rang out in the direction of Santes. From the booming roar above me I knew that 'Long Hans' had intervened in the fighting. Before I reached Fournes, the artillery stopped and I heard heavy machine-gun fire, rifle fire and mines. Our troops had gone on the attack. This trench battle did not last long, however, because shortly afterwards the artillery went back into action again.

Sergeant Umann had no messages for me when I entered and allowed me to remain in Fournes. Adolf Hitler and his comrades were still in the trenches. About 10 o'clock, others came back to the quarters dead tired. Hitler's uniform looked as if he had bathed in mud, he said not a single word, drank his tea and, having eaten a piece of bread and jam, threw himself down on his bed. Not until the next morning did he say anything about the previous day's fighting. One could see that he was greatly troubled by what he had seen. The orderlies said that Hitler, when he heard the drumfire in the morning, jumped up from his bed and paced around restlessly with his rifle. They had wanted, most of all, to throw their boots at his head because when one heard the shooting at the front, no man could sleep any longer.

All the same, we were all glad that the attack had been carried off so successfully. The iron wall which our division formed at Fromelles was not so easy to break through.

Night Bath in the Castle Moat at Ligny

On 27 September 1915 towards evening, I rode with a message to Division at Houbordin. Night had already fallen when I arrived, I could hardly see my hand in front of my eyes, and it was raining heavily when I rode back with a new message from division staff. At the entrance to the village in front of a cafe, many Prussian drivers stood by their wagons around a burning lantern and drank from a bottle of schnapps. They had already had quite a bit to drink and swayed alarmingly. One of these drivers recognised me and called to me, 'Ghost Rider, come here, I have known you for a long time, you are a dashing horseman. We'd like to share a drink with you.' They offered me a full mug, however, they drank quickly and I soon noticed that they weren't allowing me to keep up. I refused to drink any more and rode off.

After a short while the cognac was taking effect and the whole of France was dancing around me. In the only hostel which stood on the road, I got some water from the landlady to dampen the effect of the schnaps. With this, my head was clearer. I rode cross-country by a light in the direction of the castle where I had to give my message. Suddenly my horse stood still. I tried everything to make her go forward but she neither wanted to turn right or left. I became angry at this disobedience, I gave her the spur, my horse reared up and leapt into the castle moat. At this death jump, I fell out of the saddle. If I had not been desperately holding on to my horse by the neck, I would have fallen to my death. The animal was not intoxicated like its rider and swam like a fish around the moat and up to the castle bridge. There I heard voices and called for help. The people heard me and answered, one of them using a torch to illuminate the moat along to the steps. I pulled my horse around and before I could swing out of the saddle she had reached the bottom steps and moved with a powerful jump upwards. In the meantime, the entire castle garrison came out. They brought rope and even a spotlight. When they saw me on solid ground, wet through, covered in weed in the light of the spotlight, there was a great commotion, and everyone wanted to know how I had landed in the castle moat in the dead of night. However, I only answered the many questions briefly for the truth that I was drunk, and my horse had been compelled to make this jump, had to be kept secret. I gave the sodden message for the major to an artillery man and set off. I could dry my clothes at the home of one of the well-known French families in Wavrin.

Next day, my comrades already knew about my adventure and the story amused them. Adolf scrutinised me and asked whether I was also clean after the bath in the castle moat at Ligny. Whoever has been harmed need fear no mocking. From now on, this experience served as a warning to me and I never consumed alcohol on an assignment again.

Experiences in Wavrin

On 30 September, I shoed my horse in Wavrin. On my way there, I met Adolf Hitler. He was stood still observing nearby troops practising throwing hand grenades. A non-commissioned officer was supervising but Hitler noticed, as an old hand, that the recruits were very careless in the skill of removing the pins, and said to me, 'If that NCO doesn't pay attention to his recruits, something is going to happen.' After a short exchange we went our separate ways. Hitler marched back to Fournes, and I rode on to the blacksmith.

My horse was shod. Riding by, I saw, in the garden of a villa, how a batman was urging his master's horse to jump over an erected obstacle. Every time, the black horse stalled in front of the bar or reared up. The batman didn't have much luck and, at my request, we changed horses. The stubborn nag shot away quickly over the bar. It was a good high jumper. I put the bar up to 1.70m, and it achieved this with ease. Now I asked the batman to clear the obstacle. At first, he didn't want to but, with his comrades watching on, he agreed. We rode up to the obstacle, the black horse jumped, only this time it threw its rider off in front of his friends. The batman flew out of the saddle when my horse prepared to jump, which caused great laughter among the spectators. He threw angry looks at me and, ignoring me, led his horse away from the site of the competition. My horse picked the pockets of those there and got plenty of bread and sugar. Luckily, I had showed some riding skill and set out on the way to Fournes.

Just behind Wavrin I heard that the recruits were once again practising with hand grenades. All at once a blood-curdling cry rang out. One of the recruits sprang up from the field and waved. I raced towards him and when I reached him, he collapsed unconscious streaked in blood. Now I knew what had happened and rode to the exercise yard. On a mound, many of the recruits were writhing in their own blood, one of them was already dead. The face of the NCO, already an old man, was just a lump of meat; he was dead. Only two of those men practising got away with light injuries.

As fast as possible I raced to the field hospital to advise the chief doctor. The latter immediately sent an ambulance with a doctor to the site of the unfortunate accident. Most of them paid for their wounds. Seven dead and two dying were brought to the hospital. The misfortune happened because one recruit, when they were standing together, handled one of the grenades without care and it exploded suddenly. Immediately afterwards, when I told Hitler what had happened, he wasn't surprised but reflected, 'With such thoughtless handling by the men as I saw this morning, that could not fail to happen. The NCO should have been aware that there were hand grenades in their hands not eggs.'

On the subsequent day I was sent to Fromelles with a message from Dr Dir. Hitler and a second messenger went the same way. The road from

Fournes to Fromelles was heavily bombarded and I had soon overtaken both of them. Hitler, when I came past, as usual, made his fine bow, he was in good spirits and we exchanged a few humorous words as soldiers do. In Fromelles I gave my message to the medical sergeant and could no longer see Hitler and W. They must have turned off the path. Then I heard enemy shooting. At the same time a shell exploded on the road where a single infantry man was marching. He was flung into the air and my horse reared up in terror. The poor chap was already dead, his face burned as black as coal and also a foot torn off. I immediately searched for men who could carry the dead man to their quarters.

It occurred to me whether on this path, where, since March, this was the third time something similar had happened, Hitler or I would meet our fate.

Penetration of the English

Having bloodily thrown back the attack of the English on 25 September between Fromelles and Radinghem, our enemy moved their focal point against the left flank of 7th Corps between Hullust and Loos, achieving an advance with a breadth of 6½km forward and 2km deep into our front. The left flank of 7th army corps, south of the canal at La Bassée, was already strongly threatened. As a result, different battalions were combined and, under the command of First Lieutenant Staubwasser, were sent there. The combined regiment had the objective of clearing mine no. 8 and the Hohenzollern Redoubt. On 2 October, our regiment was relieved by a battalion, the latter composed of two other companies of our regiment.

We were sitting drinking coffee on the morning of 2 October when the order reached us. The orderlies had to go. Hitler wasted no time in eating his bread and butter. He fetched his rifle down, inspected the barrel, oiled it and in a few minutes stood ready for action on the road. 'Today he will have his day again, perhaps they will shoot his lightning conductor away from under him,' mumbled one of his comrades to him. I happened to have my horse with me and without concerning myself further with the battalion, or the orderlies, rode further via Wavrin–Don to Billy where the Hohenzollern Redoubt was. For a good 3½ hours I had to ride briskly. In Don I saw the first traces of the fighting in Loos. Endless columns of loaded ambulances came down the Grenay road where, according to the reports from the orderlies, a mobile machine-gun section had been shelled. The countryside around La Bassée was still not familiar to me so I decided to wait at Billy station for our battalion which shortly afterwards marched up. At the end of the troop came Adolf Hitler with some of the orderlies. I joined them but immediately afterwards I got the order to report to Dr Dir.

When our battalion marched through Billy there were unpleasant scenes with some of the troops standing on the street. Our men were incensed that a few companies of Bavarians had been brought in to reconquer the parts of the country that had been surrendered, while masses of Prussian formations were at rest in Billy. They had taken over all the houses, most were well looked after, many even wore moustache nets, and laughed at our troops marching to the front. One of our men was so enraged by this behaviour that he jumped out of formation and knocked down one of the coquettish French NCOs with his rifle. Those present were afraid of the wild Bavarian and disappeared into their quarters.

I rode to the dressing station outside Billy. Having arrived at the regimental doctor's, I could not be used straight away. The doctors had their hands full dealing with the many wounded. After their names were registered, the dead were taken to the cemetery at Billy. An ambulance column of seven to eight wagons was continually on the way from the dressing station to the cemetery with dead comrades. Outside many mass graves were dug as there was no more space in the cemetery. The bloodied faces of the soldiers spattered with chalk were horrible to look at. Even more glaring were the black faces that appeared among them.

When the English made their first advance and penetrated as far as our rearmost lines, an Indian cavalry brigade had tried to break through our front with a quick attack. The commander of a rifle battalion, when he saw the Indian cavalry brigade's pounding, immediately occupied both minefields through which they had to come and kept his riflemen in fire discipline. They did not fire until the enemy was at close range.

After a few minutes, the Indian cavalry brigade was destroyed. The countryside resembled a snow-covered field due to the Indians' dead horses.

Most of the Indian cavalrymen who were buried at the cemetery in Billy had been shot in the head. They were big, slim, handsome cavalrymen. At that time, if the English had managed to penetrate at Loos, the whole right flank would have been taken prisoner.

Towards evening, a doctor of 17th Bavarian reserve infantry regiment gave me a letter to a Prussian doctor which I had to take to a farm in Hullust. On the way there, I stopped quite close to the combat zone and, in parts, was shelled. The trees along the road had been shot down and barricaded the way for the approaching munitions column. In partly open ground, taking advantage of every piece of cover, these columns of vehicles attempted to reach the batteries, as far as possible, by a roundabout route. Just behind Billy, on the main street which led via Loos to La Bassée–Grenay, lay many shot-up wagons with dead horses.

At 6 o'clock in the evening a fierce artillery barrage set in on mine no. 8. Our battalion had to proceed to the attack because between the nerve-wracking artillery fire and exploding mines, machine guns rattled. Our artillery was silent during the gun fire; however, the heavy shells tore through the air howling and rumbling. On the way to the next dressing station, I met a Prussian artillery major. His helmet was shot through, blood flowed continually down his face and his hair was matted with blood. As he had not been able to treat his wounds, he asked me to help him. I tied my horse to his and bandaged him up. The top of his skull was ripped open deeply. With a mutual handshake we went our separate ways, and I rode on in the direction of Hullust.

At nightfall, I stumbled on a small, shot-up farm behind which a Prussian battery was firing. The guns were built into the farm and elaborately camouflaged against aeroplanes. In a nearby chapel, stretcher bearers stood with wounded radio men and artillery men. On the altar lay an artillery man covered with a canvas sheet as if sleeping, but when the orderly lifted it I saw in his peaceful countenance a dead man. Although it was dark, I could still, through the masses of shrapnel and densely packed flaming bursts of fire, make out the combat zone. The sky was blood-red from the fires of the many shot-up houses and factories. Comrades coming from the front warned me off going further forward because I was already in range of the English machine guns, so I turned my horse round in the direction of La Bassée and travelled to a building where the flames rode high. A Prussian trooper showed me the way to Hullust. Soon I had reached my objective and I could give my message to the Prussian divisional doctor. It looked even worse here than in Billy, the friendly Prussians fed me from their field canteen and I quickly helped myself because all day I had had nothing to eat. During the night I stayed in Hullust. Frozen to the bone, I left the barn that had served as accommodation for my horse and me before dawn. Close to the minefield, I was told by Prussian troops that the Bavarians had again reconquered mine no. 8.

Other comrades came to me and told me that our battalion was on the march to Billy and was to be relieved at the earliest opportunity. I rode there and when I arrived, our battalion was already taking it easy. It had splendidly achieved its task and mine no. 8 had been taken back from the English after a short fight. The Hohenzollern Redoubt was now, again, in German hands and the battalions of 6th Bavarian reserve division returned to their old positions in Fromelles. They could boast that, in continuous battles, they had floored a far superior enemy. Adolf Hitler had, once again, during the bloody struggle at the Hohenzollern Redoubt well and truly carried out his tasks. I heard this unanimously from the orderlies. On another day we were transported back again to Fournes and occupied our old quarters. Hitler looked really dishevelled and not up to much.

Winter in Flanders

The weather in October was still very dry but by the beginning of November the rains had set in and our trench garrison had to wait, day and night, in the trenches full of water, without hope of change. With that came great plagues of rats, on one day, in one dugout, over forty of these terrible creatures were despatched.

For me, as a messenger, it was better, but even my accommodation in Chateau La Vallée was not very attractive. The downpours, which often lasted all week, flooded the barracks and I was sometimes wet through to the skin during the night on my bed because of the water coming in. In contrast to the trench garrison, I had the chance to dry my clothes with people I knew. Again, and again, I was the envy of the infantry men because of my independence as a messenger.

In off-duty hours I stayed with the orderlies who had cosy quarters. You could not believe that here everyone was able to come and go as he wished. Here there were firm house rules and whoever didn't follow them was thrown out. Only then was he allowed to knock if he promised to improve and stick strictly to the rules, which Hitler read aloud to him with a stern face but in a very humorous way. Above all, we were always cheerful, we were not down or bellyaching. Often minds were excited by intense political arguments. At that time, no one would have been dismayed by Adolf Hitler's strong personality and his opinion was approved of by the majority.

Physical comforts like our favourite coffee and our always warm room were a further attraction for many. Everyone was accepted in a comradely spirit.

Only once I know that a certain 'K' was refused hospitality when he complained, for no reason, about the life of a soldier. He was supposed to march to the front, Hitler came, wet through and covered in filth, from there. He listened for a while but soon our Adolf lost his patience and badgered him in such a way that he hurried him out of the room. We didn't see him again. If Adolf Hitler had nothing good to say about troops from the front lamenting the situation there, so he had even less time for those people remaining in the communications zone who we had the habit of naming 'Duds'. Hitler knew that even troops who had to be in the communications zone didn't complain about it like the majority of front-line troops, but he ignored them. He had the same opinion as those who were busy on the home front.

In the twenty-three months that I was around him, he did not once go on leave, never came to a hospital and had only been to Lille for half a day. His field of expertise was always on the firing range. Since October 1914, he had always slept peacefully in bed. One of the orderlies then went home so he had to take over his duties. Although he didn't have parents and was an Austrian serving in the German army, he was also, to a certain extent, homeless so there was no question of him going on leave. His life was about carrying out of his duty. At best, he occupied himself during his free time with politics, art and the study of literature.

December dawned and static warfare in our section of the front carried on in the same way. The construction of the trenches continued, and the work typically connected with that did not stop. Collapsed pieces of trench were reconstructed, the dugouts concreted and, as far as possible, made safe from shelling. The artillery fought each other, and the skirmishes and armed attacks didn't change the general position. The flooded land at Fromelles would have made any attack pointless. In the cold, wet winter of 1915/1916, the health of our troops in the trenches suffered a lot and apart from the daily wounded, many had to go to the sick bay and the worse cases were sent to hospital. Even Adolf Hitler became ill in December 1915. He looked as if he was suffering and coughed heavily but none of us, his comrades, could have convinced him to report to the doctor and he did his duties with no consideration for his ill-health. Then, when he came back at night from the front, as so many other times, he laid down with wet clothes on the woollen blanket on his wooden bed.

Now and again, relieved companies came to Chateau La Valleé for some days of rest but, even there, the men had no opportunity to dry out. So many lay in wet clothes with a high temperature on their damp beds in the barracks. Here there was only space for a few to hang up their uniforms so the majority marched back to the front in the same damp clothes. Impregnated with earth and mud, these threadbare uniforms offered no more protection to the body against the cold. Mass disease was the unavoidable consequence and whole companies had to be listed as ill by the doctor. The only advantage that our troops had during the wet season was that they didn't need to fear any attack by the enemy as their conditions were the same as ours.

It always was the infantry man who had to feel the terror of war the most. He was hungry, thirsty, cold, wet, exposed the most to enemy fire and could only be relieved by illness, wounds or death. If one was fortunate enough to come to the communications zone for a day in this condition, they were named 'the filthy front pig' by one of these clean-shaven and well-uniformed communication zone males. Even I once had a clash with one of these well-fed communication zone pigs.

Trip into the Communications Zone

I visited Lille with some comrades and those who had been discharged from the hospital. While we paused in front of a shop window in the Rue Faidherbe and admired the displays, one of the infantrymen standing nearby was suddenly approached by a spruced-up sergeant major who was in the company of a very well-powdered French woman and ordered him in brusque tones to salute him. The infantry man carried out this request quite slowly at which he was roared at, 'You living pile of filth, kindly stand still, you believe, perhaps, that it is like the trenches here. I will soon teach you to get your act together.' The infantryman, a Bavarian Swabian, immediately composed himself and said to the fat sergeant major, 'Sergeant, I was in the trenches and got filthy there, you can clean me up willingly with all the Belgian girls running around, it won't look bad on you. You must go with us once, then you will not look so smug.' The sergeant major became ever angrier and wanted us to remain standing to attention. Now I tackled him. I asked him whether he had already been to the trenches, 'Shut your mouth' was his reply. We assumed because of his angry behaviour and demeanour – such a threatening manner – that the French cocotte grabbed him by the arm and tried to push him away with the words, 'Be careful, those Bavarians are so evil.' He commented to himself when he was further away that he didn't want anything more to do with the stand-off and cleared off. It was also high time for him, as even more front-line troops had congregated around us. In the following days, I recounted, in Fournes, the incident with this communication zone pig. Adolf Hitler was pleased about his just put-down and regretted that he had not been with us.

A second incident happened to me in Santes with a railway battalion. I was supposed to buy something in the canteen for our regimental doctor. When I stepped into the yard an officer met me, I gave the stipulated salute of the cavalry (sitting to attention in the saddle). But this wasn't enough for him because he remarked, 'It appears you don't need to salute me.' I replied to him that I would have done anyway. Then he bellowed at me, 'Then at least lay your hand on your cap.' Now I could hardly suppress a laugh for I noticed that I was dealing with a bloody beginner, upon which I dared to ask him how a cavalryman was supposed to salute on a horse. Whether I perhaps was supposed to remove my cap or whether I was supposed to say, 'I have the honour to wish you good day.' This question clearly irritated him further because he wanted to salvage his honour as he yelled at me, 'Remove your cap.' I took the greatest delight in this order and the smiling faces of the soldiers standing nearby reassured me that this regulation savvy gentleman would be the target of their mocking for even longer.

In the communications zone, very many Jews were 'busy'. I must use 'busy', for a soldier's duty has nothing much to do with achievements. We had, in the List regiment, many officers of Jewish origin. The majority were, in their civilian occupation, businesspeople or students. In view of their education, they were very quick with it when they were promoted in the company. They understood very well that they should put their higher earnings up in lights especially when a decoration or promotion was to be expected in the future. But also, in our regiment, there were many Jewish soldiers who, already some months ago, had been transferred to more pleasant duties while enough Christian academic, educated comrades with much greater achievements were passed over.

The Jews had also shown themselves in the war to be good businessmen and understood perfectly how to extract from the unpleasantness the most pleasant and most useful. A Jewish company commander with whom I talked about unfairness with promotions said to my face, shortly before Christmas, 'If only in the regiment there was a superior Jewish officer then all one's Jewish subordinates would have, in their pockets, the criteria to be an officer.' He showed me his tunic and added, 'See this cross? I don't really want it for I remember nothing of the heroic deeds I have achieved. Weeks ago, on the recommendation of a good acquaintance, the Jewish adjutant, "G", of my regiment, I was suggested for promotion by my lieutenant and, shortly afterwards, received the Iron Cross, First Class. Justification is everything, and when I put my name to the validation statement, it was accepted as fact. Do you know, this tunic is a licence?' he added as he pointed to his lieutenant's tunic with an ironic smile.

In line with military discipline, Hitler always behaved correctly towards the Jewish officers, but he hated them. I only remember one incident in which Hitler, in my absence, could have grievously harmed himself.

One December morning, I met Adolf Hitler on the road to La Vallée. While we talked, we saw our Jewish adjutant 'G' approaching us and as Adolf Hitler didn't want to salute him, he jumped behind the stump of a poplar tree. However, he had been seen by the officer, so should answer to him and why he was dodging him, but Hitler just looked at him. The expression on his face, however, appeared to say more because the snooty 'G' irritated him even more, and with the threat that he would sentence him to punishment, he rode on. When Hitler came up to me again, he said, 'This Jew, I only know as an officer on the firing range. Here he can give expression to his Jewish impudence, but if he really must go to the front, then he will crawl away into a mousehole. For him there, saluting is a triviality.' I soon saw him start laughing and he marched on in the direction of Fournes while I rode with my horse to my quarters at Chateau La Vallée.

I experienced a further example of Jewish cunning and calculation after the battle of Neuve-Chapelle. I stood with a group of our men in Salomé, where the regiment had gathered for the offensive, and we spoke of the heavy losses which the regiment had suffered during the battle.

A Jew had, firstly, lamented and began to rail against the numbers. But when he saw the commander with his adjutant approaching, he was at his boldest and, with raised voice, portrayed the battle as merely an insignificant action compared with the battles of Gravelotte or Mars La Tour, where our fathers fought and in which, in a few hours, dead covered the battlefield. Colonel Betz was naturally pleased by the calculated words of the Jew and they soon also fulfilled their purpose for, after a few days, 'K' met me in La Vallée as an NCO. When I later asked, once again, how he had been so quickly promoted, he, speaking through his nose, said, 'You know, I am a Jew and we Jews are always cunning and can become whatever we want.' When I reminded him of his heroism he moved away.

I met him again later in Houtordin as an NCO serving in a command behind the lines.

Christmas, 1915 in Fournes

When we celebrated the first Christmas, 1914, none of us thought we would have to go through a second celebration on French soil. Many of our comrades at that time were now counted among the dead of 1915. It had become a rarity in our company to see an old List man. The biggest part of the garrison was made up of later reinforcements. At Christmas 1914, we had hoped for a swift end to the war. In 1915 this thought of peace had been lost, so much so that we no longer concerned ourselves with it. A miracle would have to have happened. The password was, 'Stop, keep up and shut up!' The latter didn't always happen because the view that the leadership was inadequate was already prevalent among the troops, but the main thing, however, was, they were agreed on one point. The front must hold. They complained about it habitually, the majority still, however, inwardly believing in the final victory of the German arms.

At midday on Christmas Eve, I met Adolf Hitler in the cemetery at Fournes where he was looking for the graves of fallen comrades. He went through the rows of little wooden crosses and stood before all of those that carried the name of an acquaintance. In the third to last row lay, next to each other, some of our best friends. The latter were two academics, Count von Schwerin and the volunteer Baumann, with whom Adolf Hitler was very friendly. They had both marched out with the regiment in 1914. Count von Schwerin was attached to the quartermaster, while Baumann, since marching off, had become a batman for Regimental Doctor Ruhl. In August 1915 Major L of third battalion no longer authorised that educated people could remain in a post in which anyone could be arbitrarily placed. For this reason, the pair of them were sent to the trenches but, after a few hours, they were both killed in the dugout by a direct hit. Another day, I saw them lying next to each other in Fournes cemetery and brought them a few flowers before they were buried. Close by lay a third comrade from regimental staff; he was killed in July, by shrapnel, outside the regimental dugout. Although Hitler didn't easily allow himself to fall into a melancholic mood, his features betrayed the deepest seriousness while he stood at these graves.

At Christmas 1915 brisk fire activity dominated the front and every day there were dead and wounded. In addition, due to weeks of incessant rain, the trenches were still filled with more and more water which resulted in big losses to sickness. The English, in view of their immeasurable advantage in resources, began to shell our position with the heaviest calibre shells. At times, the shelling climbed to drumfire. When, in the evening, the troops in the trenches were relieved, there were always dead and wounded and often the trench garrison said that the most dangerous time at the front was being relieved.

Almost every time when I met the relieving company, the orderlies carried dead or wounded with them and in the local command at Fournes, you could see fallen comrades in the mortuary daily. The room was always busy, sometimes it was only some but there were also other days when the whole room was full, and the stables nearby had to be used for storing bodies. It dawned on me, when I happened to see the dead, how they rested in this barren room in their mud-splattered and still wet uniforms, bloody and peacefully transferred together with glassy eyes. A wide range of ages could be found there, near the bearded home guardsman lay the beardless face of a boy whose satchel had not long been put down.

That despite these challenges the Christmas mood was none the less joyful made one think. Not everyone was like comrade Hitler, who bore every privation with stoic calm, for which we all had the greatest respect for him. He would certainly have had enough reason at Christmas 1915 to be discontented, for no Christmas greeting or parcel was awaiting him and, when comrades opened letters and parcels in front of him, he sat nearby without taking part. Since before the start of the war, he was used to these privations.

Today, Christmas 1915, I see Hitler in front of me in our dugout. During the three days of the celebration he did not speak to anyone and we could not explain why he was so taciturn. Perhaps at that time he had taken it to heart that he had forgotten all about his homeland and was not thinking of anyone with a Christmas greeting or present, or otherwise was he peeved about something? We all took the greatest care to cheer him up. Everything that we offered he declined decisively but with thanks. When he came back from taking a message during the celebrations, he sat again with his helmet on his head, deep in thought in the corner and none of us was able to bring him out of his apathy. I, jokingly, took his helmet from his head and shoved it into the bin, the contents of which he would never usually spurn. Today, however, it was no good to him.

He performed his duties as usual in the most astute way, but he didn't allow himself to speak to anyone, not even with his most trusted allies. One of my parcels, which Frau von W had sent for Christmas, contained first-class delicacies. I offered him the best because his desolation went to my heart. I would have been glad to do anything for him, however, he accepted nothing. Adolf Hitler remained, until the end of the holidays, in silence. After the celebration he was glad and cheerful and had to put up with much teasing about the way he had spent his holidays.

The English didn't react as calmly at Christmas 1915 as we had expected. Acquiring a taste for it, as had happened in 1914 at Messines, during the conspicuous quiet on the detour around Ypres 1915, there was nothing to be observed in our part of the front. Towards midnight on Christmas Eve they began shelling our front. Our artillery did not let itself be challenged and immediately returned the fire and, while the Christmas bells were ringing out at home, the enemy cannons spat death and ruin in the ranks of our comrades. Adolf Hitler had the honour, during the shelling, to be in Fromelles. In Fournes, we were concerned about him, but he came back unscathed; he said nothing about his experience and lay down upon his bed.

In the morning of the first day of Christmas, some ambulances stopped and brought dead comrades who must have lost their lives on Christmas Eve during the shelling of the trenches. In the evening I was sent to Houbordin, with a message to Division. There I encountered everyone full of Christmas spirit. In most houses lights burned and from my horse I could also see through the windows the merry faces of the civilian population who, due to the beautiful German custom, were even happier than the German troops themselves. On the isolated scattered graves outside Houbordin and, in the large cemetery where many German dead were buried, the troops laid pine branches, with black, white and red bands on them, between the many wooden crosses. Also, little Christmas trees which someone had placed lovingly for a comrade.

In Houbordin, to bring joy to someone, I visited the French mother with her three children who I knew from Fournes. From my Christmas parcels I had placed various things in my saddlebag to prepare a little

Christmas joy for this long-suffering woman with three delightful children. When I stepped into the family's room, the little ones jumped around my neck. They still recognised their 'Mr John', as they had called me in Fournes. Now I opened my saddlebag and gave the mother the things I had brought with me for her children. The woman could not contain her joy over my thoughtfulness and said, 'You Germans are a bit tough on the outside but inside you think as nobly as we French. If German soldiers didn't take on the likes of me, I and my children would have been killed long ago.' Only with the greatest trouble could I free myself from the little ones. Again, and again, they held me tightly by the belt and begged me not to leave. With this little ray of sunshine and with the satisfaction to have at least seen a child's shining eyes at Christmas time, I rode back again to the front and the dark Fournes.

New Year's Eve, 1915

On New Year's Eve morning I took a message to Lille and a second letter to Santes. Passing the entrance to Santes, many young girls in white dresses and, also young men in black suits, approached me. At first I thought it was a New Year custom, but soon noticed a burial was taking place. In the church square, there was a large crowd of people in front of the house. There stood a coffin surrounded by many girls dressed in white with palm twigs in their hands. I remained standing near the house for a long time with my horse and observed the scene. The priest came, six young French men put the coffin on their shoulders and the procession moved towards the cemetery. The whole nature of this sad parade and the uncontrolled gestures of the French inhabitants made me feel that there must have been a special story behind the death. With my helmet removed, I rode past the coffin. Suddenly, behind me, I heard a loud cry. When I turned my horse around to see what had happened, the bearers had already removed the coffin and men were holding a woman back who wanted to fall on the coffin with all her might. 'My child, they have murdered you, lest God punish the Germans.' Only now did I understand why the French inhabitants at the funeral procession cast such hateful looks in my direction. I asked one of the bereaved why the woman cursed the Germans so and under what circumstances the young Frenchman had died. He told me that the deceased had been brought from the district command in the citadel to Lille because of a refusal to work, and there they had let him die of starvation. Later I learnt that the matter would not die down. The deceased was brought here because of consistent refusal to work at the citadel, but he would not take any nourishment and after a few weeks he died of frailty. In this way, the Germans didn't let him die of hunger, but the young man chose rather to die for his fanatical nationalistic feeling than work for us.

I rode on to Lille just as a column of prisoners was marching to the marshalling yard to be transported to Germany. Despite the strong guard, the civilian population threw everything possible out of the window to their compatriots and cried out, 'Long live France, Courage and Hope'. At the station in Lille, the escort had to hold the civilian population back with their weapons in order to be able to load the prisoners, undisturbed, onto the train. When the train departed soon afterwards, they howled and shouted like someone possessed, 'Good luck and patience!' The crowd was at last driven away by the field gendarmerie.

After carrying out my mission to headquarters, I sheltered my horse and visited the coffee house. The troops of the Lille garrison had already begun their New Year celebrations, they sat there with wine and good schnapps and flirted with charming French girls. From their conversations, they also believed they were at war. The landlady of the cafe told me, in confidence, that they maintained good relationships with the German stores and that they had coffee, wine, schnapps and the like via a certain Mr Rothschild, who was a civil servant there. How that was possible, and under what guise these business transactions were carried out, was incomprehensible to me. Surely the German army command knew nothing of these shady dealings? While I was there, a stores official entered the bar, gave the lady fine sackfuls of coffee and black tea, and was paid for it. Under such relationships, it was no wonder if front-line troops drank lime-blossom tea and satisfied their hunger with the well-known 'wire entanglement' (canned meat and potatoes). I angrily departed the cafe, fetched my horse and left Lille.

At my arrival in the orderlies' quarters at Fournes, a good New Year atmosphere pervaded. Messenger Dammerl had brewed different field cauldrons full of punch and it appeared that those present had already had quite a lot. In contrast to his depressed Christmas mood, Adolf Hitler was in a good frame of mind. He vented his high spirits, as usual, to the optimum which everyone admired him for. I could only take part in this drinking session for a short while as, courtesy of Sergeant Umann, I received a second message which I was supposed to take to Division at Houbordin. Despite my objections that my horse was tired and had loosened two shoes, Umann insisted on his order. Halfway there, my horse, as I had predicted, lost a front shoe and, to spare the hoof, I had to ride slowly to Houbordin. When I had delivered my communication I looked for a blacksmith to reshoe my horse. A blacksmith took care of this and I aimed to go back to Fournes the shortest way. But at the crossroads I lost my way and, instead of riding straight on, I turned right. Suddenly, I came upon a wire obstacle that blocked my path. It was pitch black. I fetched my torch and wanted to get my bearings on the map. But soon I heard a voice in front of me, 'Turn that light off'. A sentry approached me and was astonished when he saw me on horseback and advised me to, as quickly as possible, clear off. English machine guns were aimed at this spot so now I set off and rode at top speed back along the road to the heights where I soon reached the correct road to Fournes. Having given my response to the regimental office, I wanted to have some of the orderlies' punch but, oh dear! the quarters and the field cauldron were empty; the orderlies marched to Fromelles because the regiment stood on alert and we were definitely expecting an attack or a bombardment.

At midnight sharp, our artillery opened fire on the English front and the New Year bombardment began. The artillery battle raged for a full hour and there were, as at Christmas, many dead and wounded. The quartermasters, who had been in the firing position on New Year's night, recounted on another day that it had been dreadful, and they no longer believed that they would come out of the firing alive. From Adolf Hitler, I heard that their shelter was full of water filled shell holes, and the wet and dirty clothes were also evidence of this.

1916

The second year of the war was over and with the start of the new year we awaited new and significant responsibilities. The List regiment had, in the various battles in the war, already proved itself battle-hardened and asserted itself against its enemy which, with greatly superior forces, spared no victim and again and again was able to call upon huge resources of men and immeasurable support. Our regiment could boast having lost not one piece of trench. Also, in different places where parts of our regiment had been called upon to help, they fought every time successfully and did not rest until they had completely carried out their task.

Adolf Hitler was one of the few who, during the whole year, took part in all the regiment's battles. He had, in the static war, performed superhuman feats as an orderly in dangerous and important positions. When he sometimes shivered with fever, which made his teeth chatter and we wanted to send for a doctor, he attended to something more important or he didn't listen to us at all. One peculiar prophecy I remember in this context: shortly before Christmas, he expressed that we would be hearing a lot more about him, we should just wait until his time came. Today, when half the world talks about him, I certainly think of this remark in 1915. In the middle of January, the first Prussian regiments arrived in Fournes from the Eastern Front. An imminent offensive was expected. These troops still had no idea about the regular war methods of the Western enemy. They expected to clear up quickly just as they had in Russia. Outside our quarters, a major of this guard regiment made a remark which we orderlies, among them Adolf Hitler, listened to attentively. He expressed, in basic words, the greater persistence of the Western enemy and the particular connections to the Western Front which, in the view of the Prussian soldiers, would not diminish his innate discipline and bravery in ousting the heavily entrenched enemy from his front. He expected everyone to do his duty so he could succeed in achieving free passage in the West which, up until now, other troops had failed to do.

Adolf Hitler listened to this guard major's remarks intently, pulled at his helmet and shook his head as usual when something appeared improbable to him. After a three-time hoorah for the kaiser, the major allowed his battalion to move on. Some of our Prussian comrades asked us what it was like 'up front' and whether we had had heavy losses up to now. Adolf Hitler answered their question ironically, 'Ah, here in the West it's not bad. You have just heard that from your major. You lot can calmly leave your lathes here and take your bean canes with you and, instead of hand grenades, take your tin cans with you and throw them at the Tommies' skulls. Then you can run away.' A quite young guardsman asked somewhat suspiciously, 'But I don't understand, if nothing is going on here comrade, what do all these soldiers graves, which I have seen back there, mean?'

Adolf Hitler turned to him and said, 'That's honestly those who have shot themselves.' When, afterwards, in our quarters, we further discussed the guard major's speech, Hitler said, 'Pay attention to what happens when they advance tomorrow. I certainly expect big losses', and he wasn't wrong. The reserve guard regiment marched off in the evening to the trenches to relieve a different regiment there but had no inkling of the dangers that relieving in the Western Theatre brought with it, and they marched carelessly up to the approach trench as they were accustomed to in the East. The English had observed the marching up of the Prussians and peppered them with machine-gun fire which served to create sinister confusion. Instead of immediately throwing themselves down, the guard companies scattered aimlessly about; at the entrance to the approach trench alone lay twenty-one dead whose number grew the next day to forty-six. Throughout the night the ambulances had to go back and forth. After the application of a field dressing, the wounded were brought back while the dead were brought on stretchers to the local command. Before they came to the cemeteries, I went, with Adolf Hitler and some other comrades, to the headquarters where a sad scene awaited us. In four rows, they lay next to each other; many had been shot in the head.

In the afternoon, the fallen Prussian comrades were buried with full military honours. After the band had played, the Protestant army chaplain held a touching service for the fallen with the text 'you have fought a worthy battle, you have kept your faith, I give you the crown of life'. When the last officers present had thrown a handful of earth into the two mass graves, a captain from the guard of honour presented arms to the sound of 'To the Good Comrade' and the graves were covered over. Afterwards the guard of honour moved away swiftly.

I lingered for a while with my comrades in the cemetery. The poignant burial of our fallen Prussian comrades had awakened, in us Bavarians, a nasty feeling for never, with such honour, were our comrades buried. On the way to our quarters Adolf Hitler said, 'For these deaths, I would make their leader responsible, he who brought his troops with the joy of victory to the Western Front, not making them aware of the prevailing dangers and who had thought of being able to break through the front with a lot of hullaballoo.' These horrible losses could have been spared. Every one of us simple men would have known, through great experience and local knowledge, how to avoid this drama.

We weren't back to our quarters before the engineers' camp near the cemetery was shelled and a shell exploded quite near the burial party, interrupting their work and making them curse. Any closer and the gravediggers would have been buried with it.

An Unsuccessful Hunt

In January our brigade commander, General R, organised a hunt for the officers of both regiments. He wanted the opportunity of testing the horsemanship of the officers in his brigade. Now, the greater part of the officers going on the hunt had forgotten how to ride owing to the long-lasting static warfare and were not exactly enamoured with this invitation. Many tried through some pretext or other to shirk this so as to avoid disgrace.

On the evening before the event, Lieutenant E came to me and asked me to help him to set up the jumps. He then said, 'My dear Mend, I would really like, this evening, to be marching to the trenches, rather than taking part in the fun tomorrow.'

Next day, when I rode to La Vallée, the gentlemen stood, in full riding dress, ready at the entrance to the village which was the start. At the front rode General R who then also gave the signal to start. Major L of our third battalion rode with his adjutant as the last one. The field rode quite quickly up to the first obstacle. At the thought of jumping many horses were uncomfortable and refused. Some riders even fell off. Only General R with his adjutant and Colonel B managed to jump every obstacle and made a good finish, although both were portly, and of advanced years. However, it didn't go well for the adjutant of the battalion commander. When his horse stood stationary before the first obstacle, the commander also held his horse back and, since the time of recruiting, I have never heard so many military expressions of strength as the adjutant had to swallow. His nag stood looking at the stars, like a sawhorse before the bar, and the rider became completely panicked in the face of the constant yelling from his major. I stood with Adolf Hitler and many comrades close by and, in my life, I have not laughed as much as then. Then when the adjutant began to push and pull, Adolf Hitler each time made foot and hand movements in a humorous way. When Major L wanted, in his anger, to make the adjutant's horse move forward by beating it, he lashed out at his own and caught it a blow to the flank. Now the boss gave up and moved away saying that he didn't need such a companion. General R, with his adjutant and Colonel B, had ridden almost faultlessly, and one of the referees would certainly have marked him out for first prize. Without collecting the other gentleman together, he had allowed the participants to return to their quarters because he did not want to draw attention to the fiasco the event had become. Once the gentleman had left the field, I rode my horse up to the first obstacle where the adjutant was still trying to jump his horse. With bitter words, he pushed all the blame onto Major L, who, as a result of his yelling, had made him nervous and his horse timid. Now, I got onto the brown horse and, while the lieutenant held my horse, I rode quickly over the jump and went on to clear the other obstacles. When I again returned to the adjutant, my comrades applauded me and called out, 'Bravo despatch rider.' The lieutenant was, of course, very embarrassed about his failure, and rode alone back to Chateau La Vallée with a lowered head. Outside our regimental office, the other orderlies again paid homage to me. Adolf Hitler stood before me and, as usual, with bows and priceless quotes, expressed his amazement. I rode up to him and pushed open the doors.

Medical Service

In February it was cold and wet. The sick bay in Fournes was overflowing with comrades who had colds. The majority were suffering from sore throats and other cold symptoms which had been caught in the trenches. They were not concerned about their health; in contrast they were glad to have a roof over their heads and to be able to dry their clothes which for weeks had hung like dirty dish rags on their bodies and from the sick bay a musty and penetrating aroma radiated. They didn't think here about the danger, although only a few days ago a heavy shell had exploded near the sick bay. Shrapnel blew in the windows, everything was the same. But just to have a little dry place again to lay down. In the corner of the sick bay lay a still quite young chap who, a few days before, had been sent to the trenches. However, after a short time, he had developed tonsillitis. As well as that, he had a bandaged hand which, during his sleep in the dugout, a rat had bitten. Because of ground water and the cold, these animals fled into the dugouts and didn't leave the soldiers alone. Also, many comrades had to be taken to the isolation hospital due to typhoid developing as a result of the unhygienic conditions.

At the end of January, I had to take a letter to St Sauveur hospital in Lille. At that time there was a significant outbreak of typhus so that on one day sixty-seven deaths were recorded and the nurse told me that two of his colleagues were constantly on the move with stretchers with comrades who had died in the meantime. Many infections were caused because of the general uncleanliness. From bad experience, the care of the body was dulled, even if there was the opportunity. Only educated comrades set store by cleanliness when they were at rest. At this time I remember that Hitler called a comrade who absolutely didn't want to wash a 'living dung heap'. Although Hitler was no less vain, he set store by cleanliness and used every opportunity to keep his tired uniform and footwear in good order. For he scratched and brushed himself when he came back from the trenches to such an extent that it sometimes made us laugh.

I didn't give the slightest thought to how many perhaps think of uneducated people, in contrast, many of our comrades who listened to those educated people in civilian life were the very ones who went wild and were waited on by no servant girl. Simple farm hands in contrast took advantage of every opportunity to show themselves in a more manly way.

All these situations, which a static war brings with it and which badly damaged the state of health of troops, had to be fought by our doctors with all possible means to prevent an outbreak. In February, the order came from high command that even the French civilian population was to be vaccinated by German doctors. I had just come in to Waverines as long rows of woman and girls were standing in front of the headquarters, and the two doctors were carrying out the vaccinations. Many refused vigourously to open their blouses and be painted with iodine tincture. It was, however, necessary and their refusal wasn't really taken seriously. Then, when they left the headquarters with open blouses, they were laughing, because the German doctor who was giving the vaccine had a real eye for the ladies and had a nice word for each of them. Outside the headquarters I heard again and again, the women saying, 'The doctor is very nice and it doesn't hurt.'

Farewell from the Regiment

The English continued their expected bombardment of our position. At the beginning of May, the English artillery bombarded us with a hitherto unseen ferocity and aircraft were very active. All important points were carpet bombed, particularly Wavrin, lying about a half an hour to the rear, in which there were always reserve troops. Villages which lay far behind the front and, until now, had been spared, were now shelled almost daily by long-range shells. With the lengthening of war, weapons were also becoming even more terrible. In 1914, our infantry fought with fixed bayonets when they went on the attack. In 1916, the infantryman, apart from his rifle, had at his disposal all sorts of weapons when he went on the attack.

In March, I was ordered with some other despatch riders to divisional headquarters in Wavrin to which belonged 6th cavalry regiment. For almost nineteen months I had been with the List regiment and since marching out I had carried out my duties all this time without leave or being sick. I would, of course, have preferred to stay. Also, I worried for my horse which I didn't want to give up to anyone else. Already in January, Sergeant Umann had told me that my relief was imminent, he just didn't know on what day.

On 5 March in the evening I got the order to march with some other despatch riders to Wavrin in order to report to the first troop of the reserve cavalry regiment no. 6. I said my goodbyes to the orderlies present in Fournes. Adolf Hitler was, unfortunately, not there but I left messages for him and the next morning I rode off with both my comrades to Fournes, to report to the troop commander. My only consolation was that I wasn't far from my comrades, and still had the opportunity to meet my old acquaintances.

Even mounted troops were used in 1916 in the trenches and every evening they went up to the position in Fournes. After their relief they had the pleasure of sorting out their horses and equipment and the sergeant took care of any other issues. Major von W, my troop leader, used me as interpreter to headquarters as he also was district commander, and I would have been happy to be able to leave my horse with him. My main occupation was writing passes at headquarters and listening to the various madames and misses who gossiped together. But after a few days, because of laryngitis, I had to go to the hospital in Lille. Six weeks later, when I left and came back to Wavrin I took up my old occupation as interpreter and, almost every evening, had to ride to the front with the communications officer.

Often, I tried to make a detour to Fournes. However, on each occasion there was no time or opportunity and only now and again did I get news from my comrades there. Adolf Hitler was, once again, in post as orderly and rat burier, and daily went on his way from Fournes to Fromelles. Only this way was now even more dangerous, and not a day passed when vehicles and even teams which marched to the front in the evening didn't reach their destination because of the expected bombardment.

In March 1915 when we occupied the position at Fromelles, the route there was not yet very dangerous. Now, a year later, one could speak of luck if one came back unscathed. Finally, in May, I had, once again, the opportunity to ride to Fournes and visit some comrades. All of my acquaintances from the List regiment complained about the increasing enemy artillery fire. The quartermasters' drivers, who, every evening, had to drive up to Fromelles with field canteens and material for rebuilding, told me that if such losses in horses continued, then the regiment could not bring forward enough horses.

At the end of May, the enemy bombardment increased to such drumfire that even the windowpanes at headquarters continuously rattled. A despatch rider who had stayed with the List regiment and was assigned to the quartermasters visited in Wavrin at the end of May 1916. To my question how the messengers were and, whether Hitler, Dammerl, Jackl, Schmidt and so on, were well, he said to me they had all made wills. Fate can call at any moment, we all live from day to day and you should be glad that you are able to come back a few kilometres.

Almost every evening before sundown an enemy squadron appeared on the horizon with numerous planes and dropped bombs behind our front on the key points. They were successful almost every time and many soldiers and civilians were killed. This intensive enemy artillery and air activity made an imminent attack by our enemy expected. The troops, filled with the old spirit, were just waiting until the enemy attacked our position. They had already sent his storm troopers home with bloody heads. They had long since got fed up with the nerve-wracking static war.

On the way back from Radinghem via Beaucamp, I met some engineers who knew me well from Fournes and spoke to them. They were old campaigners and they had already achieved great things in many battles, with spars and hand grenades. One of them, chest full of medals, said, 'If the Tommies don't attack us soon, I will go forward on my own and start the scrapping. We won't be teased any longer.' At this he showed me his muscles and rolled his eyes angrily. The big scar on his head bore witness to the fact that he had already fought with the English.

Battle of 19 and 20 July at Fromelles

To unite the German forces on the Western Front, the enemy had endeavoured, since the beginning of the summer battle on 24 July, to divert our attention and strength in other directions and, again and again, attacked other parts of the Western Front to prevent bigger German troop transportation for the defence on the Somme. Also, in the section of the front of 6th Bavarian reserve division at Fromelles, between Bassée, Mesnils and at Les Motte, north-west of Aubers, the English, since the middle of June, had maintained heavy artillery fire. Because of this, 6th Bavarian reserve division expected the enemy attack daily. At midday on 19 July, against the section Rouge Bancs Les Mottes of 16th reserve infantry regiment, 17th reserve infantry regiment and 21st reserve infantry regiment, there went in a drumfire of shells and mines that swept our obstacles away and to the greatest extent levelled off the trenches. But the batteries of 6th Bavarian infantry regiment, a nearby battery of 17th and together with 4th Bavarian infantry regiment, which despite the numerical superiority of the English in guns and planes, didn't hesitate to shower the English positions and the assembled storm troops from their side with fire. From the right, the artillery of 50th reserve division and on the left that of 54th reserve division supported as well.

Thus the spine of the enemy attack was broken towards 6.30 in the evening. The List regiment, among them, Adolf Hitler as observer, waited calmly at Rouge Bancs for the attacking enemy and then repelled it with their often evident bravery and utter contempt for death. On the left of our part of the front, that of the List regiment with 17th reserve infantry regiment, the enemy had actually penetrated, but within the next 2 hours the depth of this incursion was reduced by supporting companies. However, the enemy was successful in establishing a deeper and wider penetration at Ostend near 21st Bavarian reserve infantry regiment in the direction of Fromelles. Towards 9 o'clock in the evening the divisional commander ordered the counterattack to be carried out from the left and right not only by 21st reserve infantry regiment but also with parts of 20th reserve infantry regiment and 16th reserve infantry regiment (List) and which was to be against the flanks of the enemy and was to gradually get underway at midnight. With united forces, 3rd regiment, of which 6th reserve engineer company was also a part, managed on the morning of 20 July to drive the Australians completely out of their positions or butcher them.

The prey amounted to 500 prisoners and 20 machine guns. 6th Bavarian reserve division could boast of having held their part of the front without assistance and inflicting enormous losses on the English. Although during the battle I was not with the List regiment, being in a formation on standby, experiencing all the terrible moments of battle, it confirmed to me that Hitler, as he was accustomed as messenger, despite the death and ruin brought by the firing and with dead and mutilated everywhere and shot-up trenches, carried out his duty with exemplary courage.

I am completely independent of Hitler and have no interest in celebrating him as a hero. But it is a hateful tactic of his political opponents when they put in their press that the corporal of the regimental staff should not have the qualifications to be a squad leader. I would like to note here, that I read in a social democratic paper that the writer of these lines about Adolf Hitler's ability in the field was badly informed. Many squad leaders who gained promotions, which Hitler as messenger and communications officer desired, didn't amount to much. Today I often have the opportunity to meet with past regimental comrades, who were in the field with Hitler in the List regiment as I was. Although their political views on Hitler divide opinion, they loathe the spiteful form in which Hitler tried to belittle front-line troops. Each who knew him in the field must concede that he had the opportunity to analyse the front-line soldier. It is regrettable that there are still Germans who prefer to view the front-line soldier as a criminal rather than celebrating him as a hero.

Some days after the battle of 20 July I had a meeting in Santes with a List man, who told me that during the day long continuous drumfire, which destroyed the telephone connections, Hitler courageously acted as observer and achieved much for the regiment. Orderly L told me that when, on 19 July, storm troops repelled an Australian division of the English command which attacked our position first, Adolf Hitler observed each of their movements with great calm and as a result important material could be brought up.

It is a question for the regiment why he did not become a squad leader. The regimental staff didn't want to lose Hitler, under any circumstances, owing to his bravery and reliability as chief messenger.

The battle of 19 and 20 July had again cost countless human victims. Alone in front of the List regiment's part of the front, thousands of dead Englishmen were counted who had crashed into our concentrated artillery and machine-gun fire Of the Australian division which had attacked in the first wave, only scattered remnants returned. We had also suffered heavy losses due to the day long continuous drumfire before the battle and some of my comrades, who had been with me since marching out in 1914, had lost their lives. All endeavours and sacrifice of humanity were again in vain. The enemy failed in breaking through the line of the 6th Bavarian division. He was unable once again to break into our line with his superior resources and numbers of troops.

This battle at Fromelles was the end of my association with Adolf Hitler in the field. On 25 July 1916, I was posted by the Ministry of War to the first Uhlan regiment as interpreter at the Puchheim prison camp at Munich. Adolf Hitler stayed on with the List regiment and was later transferred to the Somme and later in September took part in the bigger battles. There it was at Eaucourt L'abbaye the regiment found itself in unfavourable conditions. 17th, 21st and 16th Bavarian reserve infantry divisions followed from right to left. Foggy weather developed in the early days. On the morning of 1 October, heavy shelling set in and the attack followed in the afternoon. Every step of the enemy was disputed by a small force of brave Germans. The regiment kept them in check through short counterattacks. Despite this Eaucourt was lost. The List regiment relieved 21st Bavarian reserve infantry regiment on the morning of 4 October. The regiment succeeded in taking the 600m-wide English trench, however, it was only able with its dwindling force to hold half of it. The division commander had given up on the continuation of the attack until the 16th reserve infantry regiment took advantage of a favourable moment to bravely attack and take the whole trench again on the night of 6 October.

After a heavy drumfire on 7 October at 4 o'clock in the afternoon, a new bigger attack followed. The List regiment amounted on 12 October to only 350 guns but again this day brought a large-scale English attack. Scottish and English troops attacked in heavy numbers and in concentrated columns, led by officers on horses. But they didn't gain any more ground. Defying all weakness, the troops of 6th Bavarian reserve division sat firm as they had been ordered to do. Proud in the knowledge of this, they were relieved by 40th infantry division and over the following nights departed from the front. Adolf Hitler was wounded during this battle (5 October) and on 15 October, having lost his eyesight during a gas attack, had to be sent to hospital.

Homecoming

At the midday roll call on 5 July, I was aware that I was immediately being sent to Munich as interpreter. I had given my horse to Lieutenant Freiherrn von F, whose own horse I was using. She was in good hands here. I said goodbye to my squadron leader and travelled by convoy to Munich to the prison camp Puchheim. I did not enjoy my interpreting work there. I was much better suited to taming a horse than to censoring letters of condolence and love and again after three weeks I reported to the front as I regrettably could not be relieved.

After seven months, I finally succeeded, following repeated requests, to turn my back on Puchheim and be assigned to 1st replacement squadron of the heavy cavalry regiment. The replacement squadron of 1st heavy cavalry regiment ordered me to accompany transport vehicles to the various theatres of war. I went to Russia, Romania, Serbia, Macedonia, Bulgaria, Turkey, Mesopotamia and even to Italy.

In spring 1918, I had to go into hospital because months of staying in the cold, unheated wagon of the transport column had caused my hands and feet to suffer frostbite. In April 1918 I was ordered to Augsburg to the replacement battery no. 4, field artillery regiment. At the beginning of May I got an order to go to the reserve battery of munitions column 143 which was in position at La Bassée. At the latter, I again had the opportunity, until the ceasefire, to experience the war in all its cruelty. In October 1918, as the first time, enemy superiority broke through our position and sent us into retreat, I met some comrades from the List regiment which was fighting in our area. I, of course, enquired immediately after my old acquaintances, for example, Hitler and so on. Of Hitler, they told me that he was now the holder of the Iron Cross, First Class and how it happened. Luckily, he had got his sight back and was once again assigned to this regiment, where he more operated as chief messenger. The regiment was already heavily decimated. During the heavy battle at Brückenkopf Mondidier, Hitler had to deliver an important message. When he arrived in the trench, he suddenly found himself stood opposite a troop of Frenchmen, but he did not lose his presence of mind, he raised his rifle and ordered the Frenchmen, in their mother tongue, to surrender, for there was a company behind him and they had no prospect of escaping. The French immediately threw away their weapons and gave themselves up to Hitler as prisoners. Twelve was the number he led over to Commander Freiherrn von Tuboeuf. Many in this situation would have lost their courage. Because of this rare act, Hitler was decorated on 4 August 1918 with the Iron Cross, First Class. On another occasion the regiment was reduced to a few men. At this, Hitler took over leadership of the survivors and deployed them until they were relieved.

After the unhappy end to the war for us and a ten-week cross-country march from Flanders to Augsberg to the garrison where I was demobbed, I returned to Munich in January 1919 to find a position in my profession. At this time, as I was crossing the Rathausplatz in Munich, I met Adolf Hitler and Schmidt. It was a joy when we shook hands! Hitler was in a suit and looking for accommodation. We spoke about our experiences in the field and about our republic. Adolf Hitler was, at this time, not good at speaking about the new system but he hadn't lost belief in the German people. He assured us he didn't want to put his life in jeopardy or put his whole self in the picture in order to avenge the betrayal of the German people and the dead. He had not changed his views on revolution and was the same as we had known him for years in the field.

In 1923 I was abroad and read in the press something about Adolf Hitler. Immediately it was clear to me that it was about the portrayal of my regimental comrade.

In 1928 I was in the service of a German Duchess in Belgium. As her castle lay very close to our previous battle grounds, I often visited my earlier French hosts. Also, at Fournes, I came again to where Hitler and I had quarters together. Our earlier hostess asked me who was this Hitler who now wanted to declare war on France again, and about whom the newspapers in France wrote so much. When I told her that this Hitler, who had been in quarters here and with whom she had spoken a hundred times, she could hardly hide her surprise. I told her also that any dirty despatch rider who had stayed here in a room for over a year would surely remember her well. Afterwards she said quite enthusiastically, 'If it was him, then I don't believe what our newspapers write. He is the most respectable person that has stayed here.'

I have tried hard to publish my experiences with Adolf Hitler in the field truthfully, and enhanced with the accounts of my comrades.

And if today Hitler sees many Germans as foreigners who, above all, do not meddle in German relations, I would like to reply to this: if any German thought themselves so German that they acted and fulfilled their duty as a soldier during the war, such as Adolf Hitler did and, who nevertheless was born on a stretch of road behind the Bavarian border, then this humiliating peace would have been spared us.